CONNECTICUT GOVERNMENT AND POLITICS
AN INTRODUCTION

AF173953

CONNECTICUT GOVERNMENT AND POLITICS

AN INTRODUCTION

Gary L. Rose

SACRED HEART UNIVERSITY PRESS
FAIRFIELD, CONNECTICUT
2007

Library of Congress Cataloging-in-Publication Data

Rose, Gary L., 1951-
  Connecticut government and politics: an introduction /
  Gary L. Rose.
      p. cm.
  Rev ed of: Connecticut government at the millennium.
  Includes bibliographical references and index.
  ISBN 978-1-888112-16-0
  1. Connecticut–Politics and government–1951-   I. Rose,
Gary L., 1951- Connecticut government at the millennium.
II. Title.

JK3316.R65 2007
320.4745–dc22   2007030461

To Laurie, Garrison, and Meredith

Contents

CONTENTS

Preface

The devolution of power to state governments is the reason why this book was written. Beginning with the Reagan era and extending to the present, a vast amount of domestic power has been transferred from the federal to state governments. For the past twenty-five years, states, not the federal government, have been responsible for formulating and delivering an array of public services that at one time seemed far beyond the capacity of state governments. Devolution also energized state politics. This resulted in state capitols being the new focal points for citizen activism.

Many states responded to devolution by modernizing governing structures and expanding the number of support staff for the three branches of government. In Connecticut, for example, a sixty-seven million dollar Legislative Office Building was constructed in 1987 for the purpose of assisting state lawmakers with their daily work. The building, which is adjacent to the state Capitol and connected to the Capitol by an underground concourse, is an impressive state-of-the-art response to the new responsibilities assumed by state governments.

The first edition of this book, *Connecticut Government at the Millennium*, was published in 2001. My goal in writing it was to publish a work that would serve as an introductory text on government and politics in Connecticut. The first edition, like the present revised version, was written with college students in mind. The first edition addressed the historical tension between nationalists and states' rights advocates, the constitutional history of Connecticut, and the utility of the current constitution for protecting civil liberties and civil rights. Chapters were also devoted to political culture, party politics, interest groups, and the three branches of government. Each chapter in the first edition featured a lengthy interview with a political practitioner. The interviews were designed to supplement the contents of each chapter.

By 2006, however, it became clear that a revised version was long overdue. Within the space of only five years, the "land of steady habits" seemed to plunge into a state of unpredictability and political turmoil. A rash of corruption enveloped state and local government, resulting in federal indictments and prison sentences for a governor, two mayors, and a state senator. Even the chief justice of the state supreme court faced a legislative inquiry because of an ethical violation. A state once known for its ethical system of government was now referred to by media commentators and political pundits as "Corrupticut."

The state's two-party system, which had already been on the wane, also showed further signs of decay during the past five years. For example, in the 2006 mid-term election, Senator Joseph I. Lieberman, a lifelong Democrat, was elected as an Independent Democrat running under the party label of Connecticut for Lieberman. More generally, the political climate of Connecticut had also changed over a five year span. Known for its moderate brand of politics, Connecticut seemed to be moving in a decidedly more liberal direction, similar in some respects to the state of Massachusetts. In 2006, two of the three Republican members of Connecticut congressional delegation who were seeking reelection were defeated by liberal Democratic challengers.

The serious policy challenges that face Connecticut have also multiplied over the course of the past five years. The percentage of state residents without health care increased, proper care for the elderly remained unresolved, the state economy was less than impressive, and gridlock continued to afflict every major highway throughout the state. Moreover, environmental hazards caused by lightly regulated industries continued to threaten the state's air and water supply, prison overcrowding grew to an alarming degree, and the achievement gap between suburban and urban school systems persisted, despite court rulings intended to rectify this condition. Thus, the political and policy developments that occurred in Connecticut during the past five years begged for a fresh look at Connecticut politics and government.

The present book unfolds in the following manner. In Chapter One, I examine the historical and ongoing struggle between those who favor a more centralized and powerful national government and those who favor decentralized power and a stronger system of states' rights. This issue has divided Americans into political factions and political parties for more than two hundred years.

In Chapter Two, I explore the constitutional history of Connecticut. In this chapter, the Fundamental Orders of 1639, the Royal Charter of 1662, the Constitution of 1818, and the state's current constitution adopted in 1965 are described. I also include recent court rulings to demonstrate how the 1965 constitution has been harnessed to protect the civil liberties and civil rights of the Connecticut citizenry.

In Chapter Three, I examine the political complexion of Connecticut. I present a large body of evidence which demonstrates that the state has become more liberal over the years. Federal and state election results, along with the results of public opinion polls, are discussed in this chapter.

In Chapter Four, I focus on the three traditional mechanisms through which citizens can participate in the political process. These mechanisms include elections, political parties, and interest groups. The current health of such mechanisms is also reviewed in this chapter.

I devote Chapter Five exclusively to the state legislature. Special emphasis is placed on the bicameral structure of the legislature, the role of legislative leaders, and the procedure for passing legislation. Support staff and the Legislative Office Building are also described. The increased autonomy of the legislative branch in the age of devolution necessitates a separate and very full chapter devoted to this institution of government.

I explore the office of governor and the state judicial system in Chapter Six. The constitutional powers of the Connecticut governorship are presented, along with a discussion regarding the importance of a governor's public approval ratings for effective leadership. One will discover that the office of governor in Connecticut is similar to that of the American presidency, only on a smaller scale. The structure of the state judicial system is also examined in this chapter. I describe the current workload of the court, the procedure for appealing a case to the state supreme court, and the method by which cases are heard and opinions written. As in the preceding chapter on the state legislature, support staff for the office of governor and the courts are also discussed.

In Chapter Seven, I pay homage to investigative journalists and argue in no uncertain terms why a free press is vital to good government. This chapter also gives a broad overview of the various forms of media in Connecticut that provide citizens with political information, including newspapers, television and radio stations, and the so-called blogosphere.

Those familiar with *Connecticut Government at the Millennium* will notice some major differences between that work and the present version. In addition to revising and updating information, I have also reorganized and added material. The new text features two entirely new chapters. I also consolidated four chapters into two, eliminated one chapter, and divided one lengthy chapter on the three parts of the government into two distinct and detailed chapters. The new version adds a substantial amount of current commentary from political practitioners, but is also a more concise work compared to the first, especially because of the omission of the interviews that concluded each chapter, with an eye toward making it more focused and user friendly. (I believe that those interviews are still valuable, and interested readers can still consult them in copies of the first edition.) The new title, *Connecticut Government and Politics: An Introduction,* more precisely reflects the thrust of the revised work and suggests that my subject matter is not just the immediate present but also the history of Connecticut government – and our prospects for the future.

Acknowledgments

Anthony J. Cernera, president of Sacred Heart University, is the first individual that I would like to acknowledge, for his exemplary leadership of our University and for his key role in founding and sustaining the Sacred Heart University Press, which has published three of my books on Connecticut government and politics. I am grateful for this opportunity and very much appreciate Dr. Cernera's continuing support for my academic endeavors.

I also want to thank Sidney Gottlieb, director of editorial and production activities for the Sacred Heart University Press, for his meticulous attention to my work and efficient organization of everything it takes to turn a manuscript into a book.

Several other individuals were also very helpful with respect to the publication of this work's first edition. My friend Melanie M. Spencer offered exceptional editorial and stylistic suggestions. Former work-study students Megan Flood and Patricia Clarke assisted me in various ways with research. Loretta Winter, my former administrative assistant, efficiently assisted me with multiple production details. John K. White, of Catholic University, was also instrumental in providing feedback and insightful commentary.

While writing the revised edition, I was most fortunate to have two dedicated and industrious individuals assist me in numerous ways. My new departmental assistant, Colette Rossignol, is a terrific asset to the political science program, and her attention to departmental details has allowed me to write with focus and concentration. Teresa Fennell, my current work-study student, has proven to be a superb proofreader and research assistant. I deeply appreciate Teresa's excellent editorial suggestions and her assistance with tracking down facts and figures relevant to Connecticut politics, and thank her for all of her excellent efforts.

My family, as always, is my source of energy and love.

CHAPTER ONE

American Federalism:
More Than Two Centuries of Political Tension

B efore one explores the components and particulars of the Connecticut polity, it is important to first discuss the features of American federalism, as well as the ongoing tension between federal and state authority throughout the course of American history. This general overview should demonstrate the centrality of state governments within the context of the American federal system, and why this work has special relevance in the twenty-first century.

One of the bedrock principles of the United States Constitution is that the power of government should be limited and restrained. Heavily influenced by the writings of classical liberal philosophers, most notably the English philosopher John Locke (1632-1704), the Founding Fathers devised an ingenious constitutional system in which power would never be concentrated in one branch or one level of government.[1] Limited government was viewed as a prerequisite to individual liberty and more generally the preservation of the newly-formed republic.

The Founding Fathers' deep belief in a system of limited government is clearly reflected in the principle known as federalism. Drafted during a sweltering hot summer in Philadelphia more than two hundred years ago, the Constitution of the United States established a governing system in which power would be divided between two levels of government, national and state. The principle of federalism is among the several distinguishing features of the American constitutional framework.

Federalism and Divided Power

The Constitution, written in response to the failure of the *Articles of Confederation* (1781-88), provides the national government with both enumerated and implied powers. The enumerated powers of the national government are most evident in Article I, Section 8 of the Constitution. Seventeen clauses outline the enumerated powers of the United States Congress. Examples include the power to coin money, regulate interstate commerce, and declare war. By enumerating the powers of the United States Congress, the Founding Fathers ensured a fairly defined yet limited set of federal responsibilities.

The implied powers of the national government, also a component of Article I, Section 8, are found in the "necessary and proper clause" of the Constitution. This clause, sometimes referred to as the "elastic clause," provides the Congress with the authority to make all laws that are "necessary and proper" for executing the enumerated powers of Congress, as well as other powers granted to the national government by the Constitution. Implied powers provide the Congress with law-making authority that may be employed in the interest of implementing national powers and, more generally, advancing the national interest. Although the "necessary and proper" clause has allowed the national government to expand its authority over time, all laws and policies enacted by the Congress must still be rooted in the enumerated powers of Congress and the Constitution. Thus, limitations are still imposed on the scope of national power despite this broad and implied grant of constitutional authority.

States' rights are also preserved under the Constitution. Article IV, Section 4 of the Constitution, for example, guarantees a republican form of government to each and every state within the union and protects all states from foreign invasion. States are therefore guaranteed a representative form of government as well as federal protection.

The Tenth Amendment to the Constitution serves as the legal foundation for state power. For states' rights advocates, the Tenth

Amendment is sacrosanct: "The powers not delegated to the United States by the Constitution, nor prohibited by it to the states, are reserved to the States respectively, or to the people." The "reserved powers" of the states have served as the constitutional basis of state authority throughout our nation's history. Staunch advocates of states' rights have been known to carry a copy of the Tenth Amendment on their person at all times.

Although the Constitution establishes a federal system of government, a careful reading of this document nevertheless raises questions regarding the scope and boundaries of national and state power. Federalism is by no means a perfectly defined governing principle, and there is considerable ambiguity with respect to the division of authority between the two levels of government. Most observers of federalism will agree that gray areas exist concerning the exact dimensions of national and state power. Precisely where national power ends and state power begins is difficult to pinpoint precisely.

The lack of precise guidelines regarding the constitutional scope of federal and state power has given rise to many controversial yet intriguing federal court cases. The United States Supreme Court frequently serves as the arbitrator in complex conflicts between the two levels of government. Students who enroll in constitutional law courses are invariably exposed to large blocks of class time devoted to court rulings regarding the principle of federalism. Such cases are among the most fascinating in the field of constitutional law.[2] The tension between federal and state authority, which has persisted for more than two hundred years, has very deep historical roots.

Historical Tension

Federalists versus Antifederalists

Since the founding of the republic, clashes involving federal and state authority have been at the heart, and perhaps soul, of American politics. A recurring source of political tension throughout our country's history has been the continual fluctuations in the locus of power within the federal framework. Repeatedly, intense political disputes emerge regarding which level of governing authority should have control over domestic policies. The debate over the scope of federal and state power has historically divided Americans into two rather distinct political factions: those who favor national solutions to domestic policy problems, and those who favor states' rights and a more decentralized approach to governing. The former faction favors what political scientists refer to as "nation-centered federalism," while the latter supports "state-centered federalism." If there is one constant debatable issue throughout the entire span of American history, it has been the contentious issue of where domestic power should reside.

The beginnings of the tension between national and state governments can be traced to the bitter conflict between Federalists and Antifederalists that erupted in 1788 during the struggle to ratify the federal Constitution. Those who supported the proposed Constitution were known as Federalists. Those who opposed the Constitution, and who supported a continuation of the Articles of Confederation, were known as Antifederalists. Patriotic Americans and men of distinction were associated with both political factions. On the Federalist side of the debate, examples of leading statesmen included Alexander Hamilton and John Adams as well as the "father" of our country, George Washington. Leading Antifederalists included an array of political leaders, such as Patrick Henry, George Mason, and George Clinton.[3]

Federalists believed that the time had arrived to strengthen national power. According to the Federalist point of view, a more effective and empowered national government was needed to promote national economic development and to provide national security. A constitution based on the principle of federalism would, according to the Federalists, effectively resolve the pressing economic and national security issues that were besieging the nation. Federalists viewed the Articles of Confederation, adopted in 1781, as a seriously flawed and deficient experiment in self-government. They argued that far too much power had been afforded to the states under the Articles of Confederation, ultimately resulting in economic stagnation, inflation, ineffective commerce among the states and with foreign nations, and more generally a fragmented nation. A debtors' revolt in 1786 against the government of Massachusetts, led by former Revolutionary War Captain Daniel Shays, further underscored the frailty of American government under the existing Articles. "Shays' Rebellion," as it was known, is regarded as a key event in terms of mobilizing public support for constitutional reform and a stronger system of government. Correspondence among Federalists during this tumultuous time period demonstrate in no uncertain terms their displeasure with the Articles of Confederation and their desire for a stronger, more centralized and stable national government. Congressman James Madison's correspondence with Governor James Randolph of Virginia reveals such a perspective: "Our situation is becoming every day more and more critical . . . No money comes into the federal treasury; no respect is paid to the federal authority; and people of reflection unanimously agree that the existing confederacy is tottering to its foundation."[4]

George Washington, writing to Thomas Jefferson, expressed his grave concern for the future of the republic and his desire for a new form of government in these terms: "The situation of the General Government (if it can be called a government) is shaken to its foundations and liable to be overset by every blast. In a word, it is at an end, and unless a remedy is soon applied, anarchy and confusion will inevitably ensue."[5]

The Antifederalists, however, were deeply suspicious of the newly drafted Constitution. They feared that political power would gradually become centralized under the Constitution and that self-government, which Antifederalists equated with states' rights, would eventually be destroyed. Antifederalists, although by no means blind to the problems inherent in the Articles of Confederation, still believed a confederal form of government with sovereignty among the individual states, rather than a system of federalism, would be more effective for securing personal liberty and preventing tyranny. According to Antifederalists, eliminating the Articles of Confederation and adopting an entirely new

Constitution based on the federal principle was not only a radical and unnecessary response to existing economic and security problems, but a threat to freedom. Antifederalists therefore strongly opposed ratification of the Constitution.

Between 1787 and 1788, many essays critical of the proposed Constitution appeared in newspapers throughout the thirteen states. The writings of "Centinel," "The Federal Farmer," "Cato," "Agrippa," and "Brutus" are among the leading Antifederalist essays written during this uncertain time period.[6] At the heart of practically every Antifederalist essay was a concern that the Constitution, if ratified, would result in tyranny and the gradual erosion of human freedom. Antifederalists feared the ambiguity and flexibility of the proposed Constitution, and argued that the new national government would most certainly destroy the political sovereignty of states and local communities. They were especially concerned that the proposed Constitution did not contain a Bill of Rights that would impose strict limits on national power, and they were deeply concerned with the vagueness and elasticity of presidential power. In the view of Antifederalists, the proposed Constitution contained many hidden dangers. The commentary of Brutus, published in the *New York Journal* on November 15, 1787, captures many of the key ideas of the Antifederalists:

> In the investigation of the constitution, under your consideration, great care should be taken, that you do not form your opinions respecting it, from unimportant provisions, or fallacious appearances. On a careful examination, you will find, that many of its parts, of little moment, are well formed; in these it has a specious resemblance of a free government – but this is not sufficient to justify the adoption of it – the gilded pill, is often found to contain the most deadly poison.[7]

In response to Antifederalists, Federalists mounted their own campaign. The Federalist campaign to secure support for the proposed Constitution was most evident in the state of New York.

At the time, the New York political climate was characterized by strong Antifederalist sentiment, a good part of which was fueled by New York's governor George Clinton, an opponent of the Constitution and, according to some constitutional historians, author of the Antifederalist "Cato" essays.[8] The controversial governor emerged as one of the main opponents of the Federalist movement.

In the interest of mobilizing support for the proposed Constitution, three distinguished and learned Federalists, all of whom were instrumental in drafting and designing the Constitution, collaborated to write a series of essays in defense of the document. This historic and scholarly effort resulted in eighty-five essays circulated by New York newspapers. Each essay, identified as "*Federalist 1*" "*Federalist 2*," and so on, was written under the pseudonym "Publius," a Latin word meaning "the Public." The essays appeared throughout a two year period, 1787-88, the same time period during which the Antifederalist writings were in circulation.

To this day, the eighty-five Federalist essays, collectively referred to as *The Federalist Papers*, serve as the leading reference regarding the strengths of the United States Constitution and original intent of the Founding Fathers. Indeed, one will find federal judges who rely on various Federalist essays to help guide their legal reasoning and interpretation of the Constitution.[9] The authors of *The Federalist Papers* were Alexander Hamilton, James Madison, and John Jay, three of the nation's most prominent Founding Fathers and distinguished statesmen. Scholars of the *Federalist Papers* conclude that Hamilton is the author of fifty-one essays, Madison penned approximately twenty-nine, and Jay wrote five.[10]

The need for a stronger union and a stronger national government is one of the central themes of the *Federalist Papers*. Consider the words of John Jay in *Federalist* 1:

> This country and this people seem to have been made for each other, and it appears as if it was the design of Providence, that an inheritance so proper and convenient

for a band of brethren, united to each other by the strongest
ties, should never be split into a number of unsocial, jealous,
and alien sovereignties.[11]

Although the authors of *The Federalist Papers* adamantly
defended the powers of the proposed central government and the
concept of a strong union, it should be noted that "Publius" also
recognized the importance of state governments and states' rights.
State power would undoubtedly be diminished under the proposed
Constitution, but state governments, in the view of Federalists, were
to remain vital units of the new federal system.

Although the Antifederalists failed in their effort to prevent
ratification of the Constitution, the conflict between nationalists
and states' rights advocates has in many ways continued unabated
for well over two hundred years. The Federalist versus Antifederalist
debate over the proper distribution of power is one of the most
recurrent political themes in the history of the United States.

The Origin of National Parties

The first political party system in the United States (1796-
1816) pitted Alexander Hamilton's Federalist Party against Thomas
Jefferson's Democratic-Republican Party.[12] The party system
emerged largely as a result of competing perspectives concerning the
distribution of power between national and state authority. The
Federalist Party, which included many strident economic
nationalists, favored a more centralized form of federalism with
broad national power. The Jeffersonians favored a more
decentralized system of federalism in which the bulk of domestic
power would be vested in state and local governments.

At the heart of this division was the highly volatile and
controversial issue regarding the formation of a national bank.
Federalists viewed the formation of a national bank as a desirable
mechanism conducive to economic development and national
prosperity. The Jeffersonians opposed the creation of a national
bank on the grounds that such an institution would destroy state

banking interests and eventually states' rights. Party loyalties during the early days of the republic were heavily conditioned by perspectives regarding the desirability of a national bank.

In some respects, the Hamiltonian versus Jeffersonian visions of government were manifestations of the Federalist versus Antifederalist conflict that emerged during the fight for constitutional ratification. However, it would now be political parties, not political factions, that would carry the banners of nationalism versus states' rights. Moreover, the two major political parties in subsequent years, albeit under different party labels, would continue to embrace and espouse the Hamiltonian versus Jeffersonian doctrines.[13] The intensity of this debate would eventually result in a tragic and extremely bloody civil war.

The Civil War: The Tension Erupts

Beginning in 1861, eleven southern states seceded from the United States and formed the Confederate States of America. Secession resulted in a civil war between Northern and Southern states and the subsequent loss of more than 630,000 lives, the most devastating war in American history. Although the issue of slavery was at the root of this horrific conflict, the war was also the end result of conflicting interpretations regarding the proper scope of federal and state power. The issue of federalism and the scope of national versus state power so deeply polarized the American people that war was deemed the most logical alternative for resolving the dispute.

Legal justification for southern secession was rooted in the controversial writings and theories of states' rights advocates, most notably those of southern statesman John C. Calhoun (1782-1850). Calhoun, a U.S. senator from South Carolina and former vice-president of the United States under Presidents John Quincy Adams and Andrew Jackson, articulated what became known as the "doctrine of nullification." This controversial doctrine placed states' rights above national authority with respect to legal supremacy, in direct contradiction of the supremacy clause located in Article VI of the federal Constitution. The supremacy clause in no uncertain terms identifies the United States Constitution, national laws, and national treaties as the supreme law of the land. However, according to Calhoun, state law was superior to federal law by virtue of the fact that formation of the states had preceded the formation of the federal government. Thus, any federal law found objectionable by a state could potentially be nullified within its own borders by the state legislature. As Calhoun put it,

> The sovereignty of the states, in the fullest sense of the term, is declared to be the essential principle of the Union; and it is not only asserted as an incontestable right, but also claimed as an absolute necessity in order to protect the minority against the majority.[14]

Calhoun also contended that the formation of the federal government in 1788 was the direct result of a voluntary "compact" between individual states. Since states had voluntarily entered into a governing "compact" with one another to form the federal government, it therefore legally fell within the realm of state authority that a state, or group of states, could voluntarily withdraw from the Union as well. In Calhoun's view, the states had entered into a compact with one another "with the understanding that a state, in the last resort, has a right to judge of the expediency of resistance to oppression or secession from the Union."[15] Such a doctrine was more than appealing in states throughout the South whose economies and wealth were built squarely upon the backs of slave labor. In the view of Southern political leaders, state sovereignty and the compact theory inherently prohibited the federal government from interfering in the internal political and economic policies of the states. Thus, the policy of slavery, as well as the decision to withdraw from the Union was a prerogative of Southern states. To understand the American Civil War, one must first understand the intense commitment among Southerners to the concept of states' rights, and, most certainly, to the controversial doctrines of John C. Calhoun.

Although the Union victory affirmed the supremacy of the federal constitution and federal law, the politics of the last half of the nineteenth century continued to reflect disagreement over matters related to federalism. Despite the outcome of the Civil War, questions regarding the legal scope of federal and state power persisted. While Calhoun's doctrine of nullification and support for state secession died with the collapse of the Southern Confederacy, party loyalty and voting behavior continued to reflect the ongoing debate as to whether state or national authority should serve the needs of the American people. Political division over matters related to federalism characterized the politics of the twentieth century as well.

The Twentieth Century

For most of the twentieth century, the Democratic Party was most closely identified with promoting national goals and national power. The New Deal policies of President Franklin D. Roosevelt initiated during the Great Depression of the nineteen-thirties shaped a nationalist image for the Democrats. Beginning in 1933, the year in which Roosevelt was inaugurated as president, big government and the Democratic Party have become synonymous with one another. To this day, many Americans still equate the Democratic Party with expanded government and social welfare programs.

President Roosevelt's New Deal, launched in response to a collapsed economy, significantly expanded the economic and fiscal responsibilities of the national government. National, rather than state and local, remedies provided economic stimulation and relief for millions of Americans forced into poverty by the Depression. As a result of Roosevelt's leadership, a large number of domestic policy responsibilities were delegated to newly-established federal administrative agencies. Several domestic responsibilities that prior to the 1930s had belonged to state and local governments were transferred to the national level. This was especially evident in the area of social welfare policy. With the passage of the Social Security Act in 1935, welfare policy in the United States shifted dramatically from state and local governments to the federal government. According to Roosevelt, national solutions were required to resolve America's grave economic dilemma:

> If I read the temper of our people correctly, we now realize as we have never realized before our interdependence on each other; that we cannot merely take but we must give as well; that if we are to go forward, we must move as a trained and loyal army willing to sacrifice for the good of a common discipline. . . . We are, I know, ready and willing to submit our lives and our property to such discipline, because it makes possible a leadership which aims at a larger good. . . . This I propose to offer.[16]

An expanded and more powerful national government, in Roosevelt's view, was necessary to meet the needs of the American people. As James MacGregor Burns notes, "Throughout Roosevelt's speeches of 1934 ran this theme of government as conciliator, harmonizer, unifier of all major interests."[17]

Support for an interventionist and powerful national government, initiated and institutionalized under Roosevelt, continued without interruption under subsequent Democratic Presidents. President Harry S Truman's Fair Deal, John F. Kennedy's New Frontier, and Lyndon B. Johnson's Great Society each promoted national, rather than state, solutions for resolving an array of pressing domestic dilemmas. In addition to instituting national economic programs, the agendas of Presidents Kennedy and Johnson included national legislation designed to promote civil rights. The issue of social equality henceforth became a primary concern of American presidents and the United States government; this development further expanded the scope of federal power. Consistent with the effort to create equality, President Johnson declared a "War on Poverty." With the exception of Roosevelt's New Deal, Johnson's Great Society was the most ambitious domestic agenda in American history. During the presidency of Johnson, the national government clearly superceded the states with respect to meeting the social and economic needs of the population. The American people looked to the national government, rather than the states, for political leadership and creative public policy initiatives.

Declining Confidence in Federal Solutions

One of the great virtues of American government is that power tends to be fluid. This is true not only with respect to the distribution of power between branches of government, but also between levels of governing authority. After more than four decades of expanding national power, Americans began to reassess the policy-making role of the national government within the federal framework. By the end of the 1960s, the period of nation-centered federalism and big government appeared to have run its course. The cost and efficiency of federal programs funded by federal tax dollars began to come under close scrutiny. Many Americans began to question the costs and benefits of several federal domestic programs, such as social welfare, as well as housing and urban renewal. As John L. Palmer and Isabell V. Sawhill put it,

> The public seemed to feel that too much money was being spent on such programs, sometimes with too little effect, and that too large a proportion of the population had become dependent on federal assistance, weakening the incentives for them to make it on their own.[18]

Moreover, it was during the latter part of the 1960s that many Americans began to express serious doubts regarding the logic and morality of the Vietnam War. In the minds of a growing number of Americans, military intervention in a remote country in Southeast Asia was a misguided foreign policy. The war began to be regarded as unwinnable and an enormous waste of American resources. The decline in public confidence was particularly acute among the nation's college population. In the spring of 1967, a Gallup Poll revealed that 49 percent of college students perceived themselves as "hawks" with respect to the Vietnam War. By the winter of 1969, this figure had dramatically declined to 20 percent.[19]

To further complicate matters, misinformation disseminated by the federal government regarding the war's progress and a so-called "light at the end of the tunnel" mentality created a serious credibility gap between the American people and those in positions of national authority. Negative perceptions toward the war, the judgment of national political leaders and military generals, and growing concerns over wasteful federal spending resulted in a dramatic erosion of trust and confidence in the federal government.

The presidencies of Richard Nixon (1969-74), Gerald Ford (1974-77), and Jimmy Carter (1977-81) did little to ameliorate negative attitudes toward federal authority. During the first term of the Nixon presidency, the war in Vietnam continued to escalate in spite of the President's campaign promise to seek peace. More than 500,0000 American troops were stationed in Vietnam during the first years of the Nixon administration, more troops than at any other time in the war's history. President Nixon's abbreviated second term was consumed by the Watergate scandal, which resulted in his resignation from the Oval Office in August of 1974, the first presidential resignation in American history. Although President Nixon had attempted to improve the efficiency of government, most notably in his domestic reform proposal known as "New Federalism," and despite his masterful success in establishing diplomatic ties with Red China, trust and confidence in the federal government continued to plummet.

Trust continued to decline during the Ford and Carter administrations as well. President Ford's highly controversial pardon of President Nixon cast a cloud of suspicion over the Ford presidency. Many accused Ford of cutting a private deal with Nixon, thereby allowing the former president to escape federal prosecution. Although it was never proven that a pardon had been prearranged prior to Nixon's resignation, Ford's decision to pardon the disgraced president was nevertheless viewed by many as yet another reason not to trust the federal government.

President Carter, elected in the aftermath of the Watergate scandal, pledged to restore trust and confidence in the presidency and the national government. However, despite high hopes on the part of the American electorate, Carter's ineffectiveness as a domestic and foreign policy leader did little to reverse the public's negative perception of the federal government. Carter's failed attempts at reforming energy policy, an economy racked by inflation, and American embassy personnel held hostage in Tehran for more than a year only served to reinforce the public's antipathy toward the federal government. By 1980, trust and confidence in the federal government had declined to alarmingly low levels. The following table documents this trend.

Table 1
Trust in the National Government

	1964	1968	1972	1976	1980
Percent Saying:					
Always/Most of time	76	61	53	36	33
Some of the time	22	36	45	61	63

Source: Steffen W. Schmidt, Mack C. Shelley, II, and Barbara Bardes, *American Government and Politics Today* (Belmont, CA: Wadsworth, 1997), Table 7-2, p. 233. Question: How much of the time do you think you can trust the government in Washington to do what is right: just about always, most of the time, or only some of the time? Data based on *New York Times*/CBS News Surveys, the University of Michigan Survey Research Center, National Election Studies, and the Washington Post/Kaiser Family Foundation. Reprinted with permission.

As the data reveal, trust in the national government from 1964 to 1980 plummeted precipitously. In 1964, three-quarters of the American adult population expressed trust and confidence in the nation's central government. By 1980, this figure had declined to a mere one-third of the adult population. It is evident that perceptions of wasteful federal spending, the war in Vietnam, Watergate, a controversial pardon, and ineffective presidential leadership had seriously altered perceptions of Americans toward their national governing institutions. There can be no denying that attitudes shifted in dramatic fashion during this time period. In light of such a trend, it should come as no surprise that by 1980 the conservative political rhetoric of Ronald Reagan, the Republican nominee for president, appealed to millions of Americans. Reagan's strong support for states' rights, combined with relentless criticism of federal power, effectively connected with the American electorate. Although the Republican Party's support for states' rights had begun well before the election of Ronald Reagan, it was now more than evident that the Republican Party was in fact the party that advocated decentralized solutions to domestic policy problems and the restoration of state sovereignty.

The Reagan Revolution and New Federalism

Long before his bid for the presidency in 1980, Ronald Reagan had established himself as a leading spokesperson for conservative values and states' rights. Throughout the 1960s and 1970s, Reagan was one of the most persistent and visible conservative figures in American politics. In 1964, Reagan campaigned diligently for the Republican Party's arch-conservative and pro-states' rights presidential nominee, Arizona Senator Barry Goldwater. As a two-term governor of California (1966-74), Reagan continued to espouse the doctrine of states' rights and routinely criticized big government, federal taxation, and the liberal social policies of the Democratic Party. As a presidential candidate, first in 1968 and again in 1976, Reagan castigated the growth and power of the federal government and urged, in no uncertain terms, a restoration of state power in domestic affairs.

Decentralized power, in Reagan's view, was also conducive to free enterprise and economic growth. By devolving power to the states, business would be subject to less government regulation. Thus, states' rights, according to Reagan, would directly benefit American business activity as well society in general. Even during the 1950s, well before his entry into state and national politics,

Reagan had established himself as an engaging and dynamic spokesperson for states' rights and limited government. His support for limited government was also evident during his days as a public relations spokesperson for General Electric, a position that evolved from his job as host of *General Electric Theater* on television.

Although political support for Ronald Reagan was routinely firm among Republican conservatives, it was not until the latter part of the 1970s that the ideals expressed by Reagan began to appeal to a broader cross-section of the American electorate. By election year 1980, the American people, who had lost much faith in the national government, seemed willing to experiment with a more decentralized form of self-government. While economic inflation, economic recession, and the humiliating Iranian hostage situation during the Carter administration certainly contributed to Reagan's presidential victory in 1980, millions of voters were also attracted to the theme of limited government so eloquently and charismatically articulated by the former California governor. Many Americans seemed willing to experiment with Ronald Reagan's "New Federalism," as noted by George E. Peterson:

> One of the president's most consistently articulated criticisms has been that the national government has usurped responsibilities and authority that belong to the states. He entered office promising to redress this imbalance by setting the states free to pursue their own policy goals under their own management and by bringing government "closer to the people."[20]

"Devolution" was the term that became synonymous with the Reagan presidency, meaning, quite simply, the transfer or return of federal domestic responsibilities to state and local levels of government.[21] To "devolve" governing power is to reverse the direction in which power has "evolved." With his inauguration in 1981, devolution clearly became one of the main priorities of President Reagan's domestic agenda. Reagan's commitment to devolution was more than evident in his inaugural address of

January 20, 1981, delivered with eloquence on the western, not eastern, steps of the nation's Capitol:

> Our government has no power except that granted it by the people. It is time to check and reverse the growth of government which shows sign of having grown beyond the consent of the governed. It is my intention to curb the size and influence of the federal establishment and to demand recognition of the distinction between the powers granted to the federal government and those reserved to the States or to the people. All of us need to be reminded that the Federal Government did not create the States; the States created the Federal Government.[22]

The Reagan administration's attempt to devolve power could be observed in a number of policy areas, including but not limited to social services, business regulation, judicial power, and the manner in which federal grant money would be managed. For example, in fiscal year 1982, the Reagan administration consolidated seventy-six federal categorical grant programs into nine large block grants. By consolidating categorical grants into these block grants, Reagan intended to provide individual state governments with more discretion and flexibility over the control and expenditure of federal money.[23] Although federal guidelines still accompany block grants, such guidelines are broad and general, unlike the stringent, tightly-defined guidelines associated with categorical grants.

While it is beyond the scope of this work to empirically evaluate the success of President Reagan's attempt to establish a new model of federalism, most observers are willing to agree that a new trend in federal and state relations did commence with his election. State governments were substantially revitalized, and states, as units of the American federal system, seemed to acquire new life and energy. David Osborne, a domestic policy advisor to President Clinton and author of *Laboratories of Democracy*, offered this perspective on the Reagan era:

The 1980s have been a decade of enormous innovation at the state level. For those unfamiliar with state politics – and given the media's relentless focus on Washington, that includes most Americans – the specifics are often startling.[24]

According to Osborne, the creation of public investment funds for the purpose of providing business loans, technological innovation, reforms in public education, the emergence of collaborative tripartite arrangements between management, labor, and government, as well as the revitalization of regional industries are policy areas where states have demonstrated exceptional innovation and creativity in recent years.[25]

In *Goodbye to Goodtime Charlie*, a penetrating work concerning innovative trends in state leadership, Larry Sabato summarized the Reagan era in these terms: "The most significant of the patterns is that the states, responsible in good part for their own earlier federal ostracization, have begun to fulfill their proper role in the federal scheme of government."[26] According to Sabato, in recent years states have acquired "the will to act, to cooperate, and at the same time to compete with the national government for power and responsibility."[27] In addition to the emergence of professional and efficient state governors, other trends identified by Sabato include the development of efficient and modern state legislatures, revitalized two-party competition at the state level, and the transformation of the National Governor's Conference from a largely symbolic organization into a powerful voice on behalf of state governments.[28]

The trend toward states' rights continued under President George H.W. Bush (1989-93), yet another Republican president supportive of state-centered federalism, as well as under President William J. Clinton (1993-2001), the first Democratic president in many decades who looked favorably on the governing authority and potential of states' rights. Clinton's commitment to states' rights marked a dramatic departure from the agenda of previous Democratic presidents and further revealed his serious effort to redefine the goals and priorities of the Democratic Party. To argue that the Democratic Party under Clinton's leadership had become a states' right party similar to that of the Republican Party would be misleading, although it was clear that under Clinton's leadership, the Democrats exhibited an uncharacteristic appreciation for the place of states within the federal framework. Clinton's approval of a sweeping welfare reform bill in 1996 returning a vast amount of welfare control to state governments suggested a fresh perspective toward states' rights on the part of the Democratic Party. The bill was described as the most comprehensive reform effort with respect to the delivery of social services since the passage of the Social Security Act in 1935. Although the welfare reform bill reflected the efforts of congressional Republicans who had won control of the House of Representatives in 1994, it was nevertheless a Democratic President who eventually supported this legislation and who signed it into law.

The Twenty-First Century and President George W. Bush

The political rhetoric of Republican President George W. Bush, inaugurated on January 20, 2001, suggested a continuation of presidential support for state power and state experimentation, although there are legitimate reasons to question the President's commitment to decentralized government. The war on terror (which commenced following the devastating terrorist attacks on September 11, 2001) inevitably resulted in a more powerful federal government, and critics of the Bush Administration have suggested that such power has expanded well beyond constitutional limits. The PATRIOT Act, for example, vastly expands the domestic surveillance power of the federal government over private citizens, which raises questions about President Bush's commitment to limited government. Under the Bush Administration, the Department of Homeland Security was also established, thus bringing the number of federal cabinet departments to fifteen, and billions of dollars have been spent by the federal government to support a controversial war in Iraq. Moreover, President Bush's educational reform initiative known as "No Child Left Behind" imposes federal mandates on local schools across the land, which further calls into question this Republican President's support for state sovereignty. Additionally, efforts by the Bush Administration, along with many Republicans in Congress, to keep an incapacitated woman, Terri Schiavo, alive through a forced feeding tube, over the objections of her husband, continued to contradict the Republican Party's rhetorical insistence on limited government. As federalism scholar John Kincaid notes: "Despite having a governor, George W. Bush, in the White House, the federal system has not been a more congenial environment for the states."[29]

Nevertheless, despite apparent contradictions between President Bush's political rhetoric and federal policy, the fact of the matter is that American government is still in a decentralized mode. The current vitality of states continues to reflect in many ways the historic Reagan Revolution and President Reagan's vision of devolution. During the first decade of the twenty-first century, most of the innovative and creative domestic policy-making within the federal framework continues to take place at the subnational level of the political system. Within this decentralized era of federalism, state legislatures, state governors, and state judicial systems have assumed enlarged and vitally important roles. Special interest groups and lobbyists, not surprisingly, have also multiplied at the state level and their presence is more pronounced in the halls and committee rooms of state capitols.

State constitutions have also acquired new life in an age of devolved power. So important have state constitutions become in recent years that one would be remiss in a work on state government not to devote considerable attention to such vital documents. The Connecticut Constitution is therefore the focus of Chapter Two.

Notes

1. The seminal work of John Locke which has direct bearing on the American political tradition and constitutional framework is clearly Locke's *Second Treatise on Civil Government* published in 1689, the same

time period during which Great Britain was involved in its own revolution, known as "the Glorious Revolution." Although Locke's writings were not by any means the only intellectual influence on the perspectives of the Founding Fathers, he nevertheless occupies a very special place among those philosophers whose works served as theoretical underpinnings of the Declaration of the Independence and the U.S. Constitution.

2. A plethora of U.S. Supreme Court rulings exist regarding federal and state disputes. For many years, the high court sided with the national government and interpreted the implied powers and commerce power of Congress very broadly, thus allowing the national government to regulate a range of economic activity which at one time belonged exclusively to the states. An example of a court ruling reflective of this judicial perspective would be *U.S. v. Darby* 312 U.S. 100 (1941). In recent times, the Court has taken a more restricted view of Congress' power to regulate economic activity within the states and has issued rulings that are favorable towards the states. *U.S. v. Lopez* 514 U.S. 549 (1995) would be a prime example of the Court's restricted view of national power *vis-à-vis* the states.

3. Herbert J. Storing suggests that far too little attention has been devoted to the Antifederalists. In Storing's view, Antifederalists, although "champions of a negative and losing cause" should still be considered among our nation's Founding Fathers. Arguments presented by the Antifederalists against the proposed Constitution, according to Storing, did influence the debate over the Constitution and in some instances found their way into the Constitution itself. The Bill of Rights, for example, can be attributed to the insistence of the Antifederalists on a set of defined rights that would limit the power of the federal government. For a synthetic treatment of the Antifederalists, see Herber J. Storing, ed. *The Anti-Federalist: Writings by the Opponents of the Constitution* (Chicago: University of Chicago Press, 1981), pp. 1-5.

4. "Madison to Randolph, February 25, 1787," in *The Debates of the Several State Conventions*, ed. Jonathan Elliot, 2nd ed. (New York: Franklin, Burt Publishers, 1888-96), 5:107. Correspondence quoted in Richard M. Pious, *The American Presidency* (New York: Basic Books, 1979), p. 19.

5. "Washington to Jefferson, May 30, 1787," *The Papers of Thomas Jefferson*, Julian Boyd et al., eds. (Princeton: Princeton University Press, 1955), 9:389. Correspondence quoted in Pious, *The American Presidency*, p. 20.

6. A collection of Antifederalist writings can be found in Storing, *The Antifederalist*.

7. Storing, *The Antifederalist*, p. 122.

8. In practically all accounts of the fight to ratify the Constitution, Governor George Clinton of New York is identified as the author of the "Cato" essays.

9. In my class on constitutional law, I make it a point when covering executive powers of discussing the federal district court ruling of *Murphy v. Ford* 390 F. Supp. 372, 1374, U.S. District Court, Western District of Michigan, 1975), in which Chief Judge Fox relied on the *Federalist Papers* to uphold President Ford's controversial pardon of President Nixon. In Fox's view, the President's pardon power, defended by Alexander Hamilton in *Federalist* 74, was intended to heal the nation in the aftermath of an insurrection. The Watergate crisis, in Fox's view, was tantamount to an internal insurrection, and thus justified broad use of the pardon power on the part of the President.

10. Benjamin F. Wright, ed., *The Federalist: The Famous Papers on the Principles of American Government* (New York: Barnes and Noble, 2004).

11, John Jay, *Federalist* 2, in Wright, *The Federalist*, p. 94.

12. The development of the first two-party system is clearly covered by Paul Goodman, "The First American party System," in *The American Party System: Stages of Political Development*, ed. William Nisbet Chambers and Walter Dean Burnham (New York: Oxford University Press, 1975), pp. 56-89.

13. For a concise discussion of Hamiltonianism versus Jeffersonianism, see John Kenneth White and Daniel M. Shea, *New Party Politics: From Jefferson and Hamilton to the Information Age* (Boston: Bedford/St. Martin's, 2000), pp. 27-30.

14. Quoted in Herman von Holst, *John C. Calhoun* (New York: Chelsea House, 1980), p. 79.

15. Quoted in H.W. Brands, *Andrew Jackson* (New York: Doubleday, 2005), p. 479.

16. Quoted in James MacGregor Burns, *The Lion and the Fox* (New York: Harcourt Brace, 1956), p. 164.

17. Burns, *The Lion and the Fox* p. 183.

18. John L. Palmer and Isabell Sawhill, "Perspectives on the Reagan Experiment," in *The Reagan Experiment*, ed. Palmer and Sawhill (Washington: The Urban Institute Press, 1982), p. 3.

19. William Appleman Williams et al., eds., *America in Vietnam* (New York: W.W. Norton, 1989) p. 290.

20. George E. Peterson, "Federalism and the States: An Experiment in Decentralization," in *The Reagan Record*, ed. John L. Palmer and Isabell Sawhill (Cambridge: Ballinger Publishing Co., 1984), p. 217.

21. Peter Benda and Charles H. LeVine, "Reagan and the Bureaucracy: The Bequest, the Promise and the Legacy," in *The Reagan Legacy: Promise and Performance,* ed. Charles O. Jones (Chatham, NJ: Chatham House Publishers, 1988), p. 121.

22. President Reagan was the first President in U.S. history to be inaugurated on the west side of the Capitol. The image of Reagan as a man of the West who cherished Western values and limited government seemed relevant in the decision to relocate the inaugural ceremony.

23. Peterson, *Federalism and the States*, p. 229.

24. David Osborne, *Laboratories of Democracy* (Boston: Harvard Business School Press, 1990), p. 1.

25. Osborne, *Laboratories of Democracy*, p. 1.

26. Larry Sabato, *Goodbye to Goodtime Charlie: The American Governorship Transformed*, 2nd ed. (Washington: Congressional Quarterly Press, 1983), p. 179.

27. Sabato, *Goodbye to Goodtime Charlie*, p. 179.

28. Sabato, *Goodbye to Goodtime Charlie,* chapters 3, 4, 6.

29. John Kincaid, "Trends in Federalism: Continuity, Change and Polarization," in *Book of the States* (Lexington: The Council of State Governments, 2004), 36:21.

CHAPTER TWO

Constitutional Development in Connecticut

State governments across the land are currently characterized by a resurgence of political energy and bold experimentation in public policy making. This is especially evident in the vitality of state legislatures, the recent emergence of dynamic and creative state governors, the modernization of state judicial systems, the organization and intensity of citizen activist groups, and the reinvigoration of political party organizations. In addition to these trends, there has been an increasing amount of attention to and reliance placed on those obscure and dusty documents which for more than two centuries have served as the fundamental law at the subnational level of the governing process: state constitutions. The extent to which state constitutions have been reactivated is perhaps one of the most fascinating and interesting developments in American federalism.

State constitutions have been part of the American republic for more than two centuries. Indeed, state constitutions have a longer and richer history than the federal constitution. Prior to the American Revolution, colonial charters granted to individual colonies by the King of England were employed for the purpose of colonial governance. When America declared independence from England in 1776, a number of colonies proceeded to draft their own state constitutions. State constitutions thus supplanted the old colonial charters that had been granted to the colonies by the King. Generally speaking, the year 1776 marked the beginning of meaningful self-government among the thirteen states. In many states, the Declaration of Independence and the writing of state constitutions coincided with one another. State constitutions adopted during this era were inevitably replaced by constitutions in subsequent years that were more reflective of institutional developments in the governing process and changes within the state polity. The Massachusetts state constitution, penned by Founding Father John Adams and adopted in 1780, is the one exception. The original constitution has continued to serve as the supreme law for the state of Massachusetts for more than two hundred and twenty years, irrespective of the fact that one hundred and twenty constitutional amendments have been added. The people of Massachusetts have great reverence not only for the wisdom of John Adams, but also for their historic state constitution.[1]

Connecticut's Constitutional Heritage

The Fundamental Orders of 1639

Unlike other colonies, Connecticut had for many years enjoyed an impressive degree of political sovereignty. Long before the American Revolution and the emergence of state constitutions among the thirteen states, Connecticut had established for itself a self-governing document very similar to that of a constitution, known as Connecticut's Fundamental Orders. The Fundamental Orders is regarded as one of the oldest self-governance documents in American history. There are those who regard the Fundamental Orders as the first written constitution known to mankind and the fount of constitutional government in the Western world. Adopted more than three hundred and fifty years ago, the Fundamental Orders is the reason why Connecticut license plates bear the inscription *The Constitution State*.

The Fundamental Orders was drafted in 1639 by farmers from the rural Connecticut river towns of Hartford, Wethersfield, and Windsor. Prior to the writing of the Fundamental Orders, issues affecting the three Connecticut towns were resolved in a governing assembly known as the General Court. The General Court, established in 1637, met periodically to conduct public business in a small building known as the Hartford Meeting House.

Many issues affecting the three communities were resolved in the General Court, including the somewhat notorious decision to wage war on the hostile Pequot Indian tribe. According to Albert E. Van Dusen,

> In the river towns many felt they no longer could tolerate the Pequot menace. On May 1, 1637, the General Court at Hartford voted to wage an offensive war and summoned ninety men – forty-two from Hartford, thirty from Windsor and eighteen from Wethersfield. They selected John Mason as commander and voted one hogshead of beer for the men.[2]

As the towns grew in size, it became clear that a more effective and representative system of self-government was required. Thus, on May 31, 1638, Hartford's Founding Father, the Reverend Thomas Hooker (1583-1646) formally proposed that the three Connecticut towns enter into a new and more structured political compact. At the Hartford Meeting House, Hooker, in what is now regarded as one of the most historic sermons in American political history, urged the residents of Hartford, Windsor, and Wethersfield to adopt a representative form of government based on the consent and free will of the people. In Hooker's words, "The foundation of authority is laid in the free consent of the people. . . . As God has given us liberty, let us take it."[3]

Hooker's personal past and pivotal role in Connecticut political history should be specifically noted:

> The son of a respectable middle-class landholder, he was born north of London. At college he became a religious radical, then a spell-binding preacher, was marked for death by the Anglican Church, fled with his family to New England, led the first westward migration from

Massachusetts to Connecticut, founded a new town, and alongside of his devotion to moral law laid the basis for civil law that launched a new nation on the road to representative government.[4]

Following Hooker's urgent call for a representative system of government, Roger Ludlow of Windsor proceeded to draft a self-governing document known simply as the Fundamental Orders. The Fundamental Orders consisted of a preamble and eleven orders, and was subsequently adopted by delegates from the three Connecticut towns on January 14, 1639, at the Hartford Meeting House.[5] Connecticut's long tradition of self-government based on a written constitution had thus begun.

The historic dimension of Connecticut's Fundamental Orders cannot be overstated. Consider two important facts: First, the Fundamental Orders was adopted only nineteen years after the Pilgrims drafted the Mayflower Compact. The Fundamental Orders was therefore one of the very first attempts at elf-government in America. As Vincent Wilson, Jr., notes,

> Particularly significant is the absence, in the Fundamental Orders, of any reference to England or the authority of the Crown or Parliament. In the wilderness along the Connecticut River, the three towns had, in fact, come close to creating an independent commonwealth.[6]

Second, the Fundamental Orders was adopted approximately one hundred and fifty years prior to the writing of the federal constitution in Philadelphia. Although the federal constitution is by no means modeled after the Fundamental Orders, it is not an exaggeration to suggest that the profound respect the American people have historically exhibited toward written constitutions can be traced to Connecticut's Fundamental Orders of 1639, for it is here that we discover the roots of the American constitutional tradition. The preamble to the Fundamental Orders not only reflects the belief of Connecticut's Founding

Fathers in self-government, but also a firm belief that religion and God should guide the course of public affairs. Unlike the federal Constitution, which would be written many years later, Connecticut's Fundamental Orders clearly merged church and state. The Puritan heritage of Connecticut's Founding Fathers is especially evident:

> For as much as it hath pleased Almighty God by the wise disposition of his divine providence so to order and dispose of things that we the Inhabitants and Residents of Windsor, Hartford and Wethersfield are now cohabitating and dwelling in and upon the River of Connectecotte and the lands thereunto adjoining; and well knowing where a people are gathered together the word of God requires that to maintain the peace and union of such a people there should be an orderly and decent Government established according to God, to order and dispose of the affairs of the people at all seasons as occasion shall require; do therefore associate and conjoin ourselves to be as one Public State or Commonwealth.

Reflecting on the Puritan heritage of Connecticut's Founding Fathers, R. Bryan Bademan, a scholar of American religious history, described it in these terms:

> The delegates who drafted the Fundamental Orders were Puritans of a similar stamp as those who settled the Massachusetts Bay Colony that same decade. Their concern with good order in society and politics reflected their deeply-held conviction that, while all of life was lived under the sovereign rule of a wise and benevolent God, the reality of human sin made communal discipline and oversight necessary for continued growth and godliness. That the Orders could be ratified without reference to the King of England does not so much suggest their democratic modernity as much as it suggests Puritan interest in the

ancient tradition of covenant-making found in the biblical texts and recently rejuvenated by some Protestant reformers.[7]

The Royal Charter of 1662

In 1662, the Fundamental Orders was replaced by a Royal Charter granted to the colony of Connecticut by King Charles II. It was Connecticut's Governor John Winthrop, Jr., of Saybrook who presented Connecticut's Charter to the King for approval. According to most accounts, Winthrop's charisma, political connections in England, diplomatic skills, and sheer persistence were central to Connecticut's success in obtaining the coveted Charter. Winthrop personally crossed the Atlantic Ocean in his effort to secure the Charter from the King.[8] Although the newly granted Charter of 1662 superseded the Fundamental Orders of 1639, it would be incorrect to suggest that the Charter actually replaced the Orders as the new body of law.

Under the Fundamental Orders, self-government had already been firmly established as part of Connecticut's political tradition. What the Charter essentially did was guarantee, rather than establish, a system of self-rule that had been in place for more than twenty years. Connecticut colonists had acquired such a deep reverence for the Fundamental Orders that elements and principles of this document were woven into the 1662 Charter. Perspectives regarding the relationship between the Fundamental Orders and the Charter are offered by two Connecticut historians. Christopher Collier offers this view:

> It is usually said that the Fundamental Orders was subsumed into the Charter, but perhaps it is more accurate to say that the Orders continued as a parallel though secondary level of fundamental law – quasi-constitutional, if you will.[9]

Richard J. Purcell, in his classic work, *Connecticut in Transition: 1775-1818*, originally published in 1918, provides this observation:

This Charter in substance was similar to the eleven Fundamental Orders of 1639, which had been drafted by representatives of the river towns as their rule of government. This similarity has enabled certain writers to maintain that the Charter was royal only in form, but otherwise a restatement of republican principles.[10]

Under the Charter the business of Connecticut government was now to be conducted in a General Assembly. The Charter provided for the annual election of an upper legislative chamber consisting of a governor, a deputy governor, and twelve assistants. The upper chamber was required to meet twice a year along with the lower house of the General Assembly, which consisted of two elected colonists from each Connecticut town. The General Assembly was given broad discretion in its lawmaking capacity, and was allowed to pass any law, as long as the law did not clash or conflict with the laws of England.[11]

Upon Winthrop's return from England, the Charter was formally presented in Hartford on October 4, 1662. In the words of W.H. Gocher, "It was declared to belong to them and their descendants forever."[12] So cherished was the Royal Charter by the political leadership and citizenry of Connecticut that the document was secreted in an oak tree when Sir Edmund Andros, a former British military commander and Royal Governor of New York, was dispatched to Connecticut by the King of England in 1686 for the purpose of confiscating the Charter and consolidating Connecticut and other New England colonies into a Dominion of New England. The Charter was therefore never relinquished to Andros and remained a living and functional governing document even while it remained in seclusion.[13]

Although Andros did establish a New England Dominion, his rule over the New England colonies was rather short-lived. In 1688, England experienced a political crisis known as the Glorious Revolution. The crisis that beset England is a long and complicated story, but in summary, the Glorious Revolution involved a power struggle between the British monarchy and the British Parliament.

The end result was the abdication of the highly unpopular King James II, and the subsequent emergence of Parliament as a more powerful force within the context of British government. The Glorious Revolution was an important turning point for the development of British constitutionalism. The supremacy of representative government and an expansion of rights for British subjects would be the end result. Moreover, England's Glorious Revolution would have a far-reaching impact on the character of colonial politics. With respect to Connecticut, the removal of King James II from the English throne weakened the authority of Edmund Andros, thereby forcing Andros to relinquish his control over the New England colonies. The events in England that led to Andros's departure from the region encouraged the Connecticut General Assembly in 1689 to formally reestablish Connecticut government under the Charter of 1662.[14] The Charter would remain as Connecticut's governing document until 1818.

New Haven Colony

Any discussion of the Royal Charter of 1662 and the political development of Connecticut as a colony during this time period must recognize the important, but often forgotten, colony of New Haven. Formed in 1638, New Haven Colony functioned as an autonomous political entity until its inclusion into the more dominant Connecticut Colony in 1665. The original six towns of New Haven Colony consisted of New Haven, Milford, Guilford, Branford, Stamford, and the Long Island town of Southold. Protection against hostile Indians appears to have been the principal motive behind the formation of the six town colony.[15] At the time of its incorporation into Connecticut Colony, New Haven Colony had expanded to include nineteen towns, the same number of towns as that in the colony of Connecticut.[16]

Although the Royal Charter officially joined New Haven Colony with Connecticut, the initial merger of the two colonies was far from harmonious. Upon learning of the merger, the political leaders of New Haven Colony were deeply resentful. They felt that the decision to forge a union had been made without consultation or consent. New Haven colonists also feared that the merger would result in a dramatic loss of power over matters unique to towns within the colony. Moreover, there was a concern, particularly among New Haven Colony's political elite, that Connecticut Colony's decision to allow freemen privileges to individuals not affiliated with a church would potentially serve to weaken the relationship between church and state.[17]

Although political tension existed between the two colonies after the granting of the Royal Charter, the various towns within New Haven Colony eventually deemed it advantageous to support the union. In 1665, New Haven Colony formally agreed to unite with Connecticut Colony, thus ending New Haven Colony as an autonomous governing entity. This is not to suggest, however, that New Haven Colony's influence within the context of the Connecticut political process was suppressed with the merger in 1665. Several Connecticut governors were chosen from towns within the original New Haven Colony, including William Leete of Guilford in 1676, Robert Treat in 1683, and Jonathan Law of Milford in 1742.[18] New Haven's political influence could also be observed with the legislative enactment on May 8, 1701 to rotate state legislative sessions between the towns of Hartford and New Haven. Prior to this, the General Assembly was convened for the May and October legislative sessions in Hartford. With the enactment in 1701, the General Assembly would meet in Hartford for the May session and convene in New Haven for the October session.[19] This political arrangement continued until the 1870s.

The Constitution of 1818

The Royal Charter of 1662 served as the principal governing document for the state of Connecticut until 1818, the year in which Connecticut adopted a state constitution. The Constitution of 1818 served as Connecticut's fundamental law until 1965, when the current state constitution was adopted. Although the Constitution of 1818 was a somewhat dramatic departure from the Royal Charter of 1662, it is important to once again note that elements of the Charter, as well as its predecessor, the Fundamental Orders of 1639, were blended into the new governing document. The same holds true for the Constitution of 1965. Thus, rather than viewing Connecticut's constitutional development as a series of new and distinct stages, it is perhaps best to approach the state's constitutional history as an evolving and unfinished story.

The Constitution of 1818 was fundamentally different from the Royal Charter in several important respects. First, church and state were now separated. The formal and legal association between government and the Congregational Church was legally severed with the adoption of the new constitution. According to Connecticut historian Christopher Collier, "Many people in Connecticut were not Congregationalists and didn't like paying taxes to support a church."[20] Thus, the long-established policy in Connecticut of supporting Congregationalism through local taxes came to an end. Tolerance of different religious faiths and sects was now emerging in Connecticut. Describing the profound religious impact of the new constitution, historian Jarvis Means Morse put it this way:

> The new constitution swept away all special privileges of a religious nature, declaring that no preference should be given by law to any Christian sect or mode of worship. Congregationalism was thus put on a level with other faiths; its ministers could no longer get together to march in procession, drink rum, and decide who was to be governor of Connecticut.[21]

A second important feature of the new constitution concerned the establishment of a three-branch governing system, similar in several respects to the model in place at the federal level. The state legislature, the governor, and state judges now functioned within their own independent spheres of constitutional authority. The separation of executive and legislative authority was an important development, as it directly enhanced the leadership capacity of the

Connecticut state governorship. It had become apparent that a stronger chief executive was needed (although as Morse notes, the state legislature, even with adoption of the new constitution, still remained the dominant element of state government). State governors were given a substantial number of formal powers, but in reality few of these powers were vigorously exercised. Prestige and custom rather than legal authority proved to be the most important sources of gubernatorial authority for a good part of the nineteenth century.[22]

The separation of the judiciary from the legislature was also quite significant. The highest organ of judicial power in Connecticut was now located in an independent judiciary consisting of a Supreme Court of Errors and a Superior Court. With the exception of smaller, inferior courts (which still remained under the jurisdiction of the state legislature), the judiciary now enjoyed considerable autonomy from the state legislature.[23]

In addition to religious and governmental reform, the Constitution of 1818 extended voting rights to previously disenfranchised citizens. Prior to the adoption of the new constitution, property requirements were associated with voting rights, and political power rested with a property-owning political elite. John Adams's observation on the Connecticut political scene concisely captured this condition:

> The state of Connecticut has always been governed by an aristocracy, more decisively than the empire of Great Britain is. Half a dozen, or, at most a dozen families, have controlled that country when a colony, as well as since it has been a state.[24]

With the adoption of the new constitution, voting rights were now extended to white males twenty-one years of age or older who had paid taxes, lived in the state for at least six months, or had served in the state's militia. The Connecticut electorate was thereby significantly expanded. With adoption of the Constitution of 1818, democratic government, albeit in modified form, began its evolution within Connecticut politics. Collier notes that the 1818 Constitution was also in many ways Connecticut's first constitution in the true sense of the term. Unlike the Royal Charter and Fundamental orders, the 1818 Constitution met what had become the "standards of constitutionalism in the United States."[25]

The adoption of a new constitution in 1818 needs to be understood within the context of three important developments: the social and economic transformation of the state itself; the steady rise of the Democratic-Republican Party and resulting partisan realignment; and the political savvy and popularity of a reform-minded state governor. As the nineteenth century progressed, it became clear to political reformers that the state was in need of a governing document that could accommodate the rapidly changing social and economic environment. Economic modernization seemed to require a new style of government with greater decision making capacity. Indeed, the forces of economic modernization had begun to emerge in the small state of Connecticut shortly after the Revolutionary War.

Approaching the end of the eighteenth century, Connecticut, unlike many other former British colonies, had experienced a dramatic economic transformation. Buttons were manufactured in Waterbury, a toll road had been constructed between New London and Norwich, banks had been chartered in New London and Hartford, and the first insurance companies had emerged in Hartford.[26] Eli Whitney's invention of the cotton gin in 1793 along with his pioneering efforts in musket manufacturing had far-reaching and profound implications, not only for Connecticut's economy but also for the economies of the thirteen states. By 1818, sixty-seven cotton mills were operating in the state.[27] Additional economic developments included a robust whaling industry in New London, gin and brandy production in Hartford County, and a silk industry in the town of Mansfield.[28] As the state's economy changed, so too did the needs of the state's population. A new constitution and a government with broader capacity seemed to be the sensible solution.

Change within the fabric of Connecticut politics also contributed to constitutional adaptation. The Federalist Party, which had practically dominated the state's politics since the 1790s, was by the second decade of the nineteenth century in a state of rapid disintegration and decline. As Richard Hofstadter notes, "party warfare was dying out altogether, as the Federalists continued to dwindle both in states and nation."[29] The Federalist Party was losing its control over American politics, including states in New England which had served as a stronghold for Federalist candidates. The Democratic-Republican Party, associated with the ideals and presidencies of Thomas Jefferson and James Madison, had by 1818 clearly eclipsed the Federalist Party at practically all levels of the political system – national, state, and local. In Connecticut, Democratic-Republican candidates were being elected to the General Assembly and town councils, and with this partisan development a new and fresh perspective towards government emerged. As Wesley W. Horton put it, "In anticipation of a Republican victory in the spring elections, in late 1817 and early 1818 the various towns passed resolutions calling for a convention."[30]

In addition to partisan change and important socio-economic developments, the emergence of the new constitution in 1818 can be attributed directly to Connecticut's newly-elected and reform-minded governor, Oliver Wolcott, Jr. Elected to the state governorship in 1817 as the leader of the Toleration Party, a third-party coalition consisting of Democratic-Republicans and Episcopalians who had become disillusioned with Federalist rule, the highly popular Wolcott was able to generate significant support for constitutional reform. Wolcott's father and grandfather had both served as governors of Connecticut, and the prestige associated with the Wolcott name clearly bolstered the governor's power and successful call for constitutional change.[31] Wolcott was a central figure in the drive for constitutional reform.

The Constitution of 1818 served as the supreme governing document for the state of Connecticut until 1965. In many ways, the 1818 Constitution admirably served as a pillar of stability for the state during periods of great economic growth, as well as periods of deep and dark economic depression. By the early nineteen-sixties however, it was apparent that constitutional reform was once again in order for the state of Connecticut. In the view of reformers, a new governing document seemed necessary to guide Connecticut through the remainder of the twentieth century and beyond. Thus, in 1965 a new constitution was proposed, written with great care, and formally adopted. At the time of this writing, the Constitution of 1965 has served as the supreme law for the state of Connecticut for more than forty years. Precisely how long the constitution will remain in place is impossible for any observer to predict. Based on Connecticut's experience with the Constitution of 1818 however, it seems reasonable to predict that this constitution, like its predecessor, will have a very long life indeed.

The Constitution of 1965

By the nineteen-sixties, pressures for constitutional reform once again emerged in Connecticut. This time, the single most important factor behind the demand for reform was the issue of legislative reapportionment. This issue had been festering in Connecticut politics for some time, and it was inevitable that such a volatile issue would result in demand for meaningful constitutional change.

The issue of legislative reapportionment rose to the surface in Connecticut as a result of a widening population disparity between rural and urban communities. During the eighteenth century and the early decades of the nineteenth century, populations of towns in Connecticut did not differ vastly. The population was, to some extent, evenly distributed across the state and among individual local communities. In 1800, excluding the extremes such as the little town of Union with 767 inhabitants, and Stonington with a population of 5,437, the population difference between Connecticut towns was at most only 4 persons to 1, with the majority of towns falling comfortably within this range.[32] Older towns in Connecticut each elected two members to serve in the Connecticut House of Representatives, while newer towns, which had fewer inhabitants, were allowed one representative each. Thus, a fair system of equal representation characterized legislative politics in Connecticut during this particular period and, generally speaking, there was little demand or need for legislative reapportionment.[33]

By the middle of the nineteenth century, however, the growing population imbalance between Connecticut's urban and rural communities raised questions of fair legislative representation. More specifically, heavily populated cities began to emerge in Connecticut, but, unfortunately for residents of urban areas, legislative representation did not correspondingly increase. The formula of one or two representatives per local community remained fixed regardless of the community's population growth. Disproportionate legislative representation was now characteristic of Connecticut politics, and the weight of individual votes was extremely unequal. The vote cast by a resident of a small, rural town in Connecticut had far more power and weight than the vote cast by a resident of one of Connecticut's expanding cities. Although there were some minor adjustments and legal tinkering with Connecticut's legislative reapportionment formula during the decades immediately following the Civil War, residents of Connecticut's urban communities remained underrepresented in the General Assembly compared to residents of rural communities. As Horton put it, "By the 1890s, the Connecticut system of representation was a national scandal."[34]

By 1900, the city of New Haven, which had grown to 108,000 inhabitants, was allotted only two state representatives, while Union, with a population of 428, also had two representatives. Moreover, examination of the population among cities and towns, when compared with the number of representatives allocated, reveals that small, rural towns in Connecticut completely dominated heavily populated cities in legislative politics. According to Horton, "44 towns, with a population of about 30,000, could legislatively overwhelm the four largest cities, with a population of about 300,000."[35]

In 1902 there was a feeble attempt by political reformers to rectify the grossly malapportioned legislative districts. A constitutional convention was convened, and over the course of five months a new constitution was written. The proposed constitution failed to win approval among the Connecticut electorate, with more than two-thirds of voters rejecting the document. Rural voters viewed the proposed constitution as a threat to their political power, while voters in urban areas regarded it as an inadequate attempt to increase their political power within the context of legislative politics. Thus, a politically unjust and fundamentally unfair system of legislative politics persisted in Connecticut for a good part of the twentieth century.[36]

By the early nineteen-sixties, the issue of legislative reapportionment could no longer be ignored by lawmakers and constitutional reformers. The issue of legislative reapportionment had now become one of the hottest political issues, not only in Connecticut, but in states across the land. Voters in rural towns were routinely controlling a majority of seats in the state legislatures. Empirical evidence during this period demonstrates serious political inequality with respect to legislative representation. In Alabama, it was theoretically possible for a minimum of 27.6 percent of the population to elect a majority of the state senate, while 37.9 percent of the state's population could elect a majority of representatives to the state house of representatives. In Connecticut, 32 percent of the state's population could theoretically control a majority of seats in the state senate, while a mere 12 percent could elect a majority of representatives to the state house. In Iowa, 35.6 percent of the population could elect a majority of the state senate, while 27.4 percent of the population could elect a majority of the lower house. Apportionment in Nevada was among the most perverse, with only 8.0 percent of the population controlling a majority of the seats in the state senate, while a majority of seats in the state house were controlled by 29.1 percent of the state's population.[37]

In addition to raising questions related to representative democracy and, more fundamentally, the concept of political equality, malapportioned legislative districts also raised questions of fairness concerning taxation and allocation of public resources. By the nineteen-sixties, urban communities were providing the lion's share of tax revenue. Unfortunately, public policies and public resources were rarely directed toward urban centers. The needs and concerns of urbanites were seldom addressed in state legislative committees or on the floors of state assemblies, despite the fact that the bulk of many state operating budgets was based on urban tax dollars. A report issued by the Conference of Mayors during the controversy over reapportionment noted that urban dwellers were for all intents and purposes treated by state lawmakers as "second-class citizens."[38]

Thus, mounting pressure in favor of legislative reapportionment was inevitable. Connecticut, like other states across the land, would be forced to undergo legislative reform. In Connecticut, a new constitution would also be written to accommodate this important objective. To more fully understand the impetus behind legislative reform in Connecticut and the writing of a new state constitution, the significance of several historic and monumental rulings issued by the United States Supreme Court regarding the controversial issue of legislative reapportionment must be examined. To understand such rulings is to understand the connection between court rulings on constitutional law and the development of representative democracy in the United States.

Initially, the Supreme Court was reluctant to become involved in matters pertaining to legislative reapportionment. In the view of the Court, the issue was more a political than a legal question, and therefore best left to the elected branches of government to resolve. The Court's position on legislative reapportionment reflected a long-standing and revered judicial tradition that maintains that law and politics should not be intertwined. Thus, for the Supreme Court to accept a case the issue must in the Court's view be "justiciable," i.e., a controversy that appropriately belongs before the Court. This is fundamentally different from what the Court regards as a "political" issue, i.e., a matter best left to the legislative and executive branches of government.

The Supreme Court's position that legislative reapportionment was a political and therefore non-justiciable issue was articulated quite clearly in *Colegrove v. Green*, 328 U.S. 549 (1946). The ruling did little to correct the inequitable state of representative democracy in American politics. Malapportioned congressional districts in the state of Illinois were the subject of dispute. Population shifts over a forty-year period had resulted in wide discrepancies between Illinois congressional districts, with a low of 112,116 residents in one district to a high of 914,053 residents in another. Those residing in the most populated congressional districts, it was estimated, had approximately one-ninth the voting power of residents in the least populated districts.[39] The Supreme Court, however, failed to see how malapportioned legislative districts constituted a justiciable issue. Justice Felix Frankfurter, one of the Court's strongest proponents of judicial restraint, and the author of the Court's majority opinion in *Colegrove*, addressed the issue in the following terms:

> In effect this is an appeal to the federal courts to reconstruct the electoral process of Illinois in order that it may be adequately represented in the councils of the Nation. . . . Nothing is clearer than that this controversy concerns matters that bring courts into immediate and active relations with party contests. From the determination of such issues this Court has traditionally held aloof. It is hostile to a democratic system to involve the judiciary in the politics of the people. And it is not less pernicious if such judicial intervention in an essentially political contest be dressed up in the abstract phases of the law. . . . Courts ought not to enter this political thicket.[40]

Malapportioned legislative districts, in the view of Justice Frankfurter, should be corrected by Congress and the state legislatures, not the Supreme Court. The *Colegrove* ruling of 1946 made clear the Supreme Court's position on the issue of legislative reapportionment: the issue was political and therefore nonjusticiable. As a result of the Supreme Court's unwillingness to resolve legislative malapportionment, political inequality continued to persist in American politics.

The historic breakthrough came sixteen years after *Colegrove,* with the landmark Supreme Court ruling of *Baker v. Carr,* 369 U.S. 186 (1962). In the years following the *Colegrove* ruling, new judges, with a decidedly liberal perspective toward civil rights and political equality, were appointed to the U.S. Supreme Court. Two appointments made by President Dwight Eisenhower were especially relevant: Earl Warren replaced Fred Vinson as chief justice in 1952, and William Brennan was appointed as an associate justice in 1957. It was clear that one of the chief objectives of the Warren Court was to employ judicial power so as to strengthen and advance the principle of equality. With a majority of the justices on the Warren Court subscribing to judicial activism rather than Frankfurter's logic of judicial restraint, it was only a matter of time before the issue of malapportioned legislative districts was deemed justiciable rather than political.

Malapportioned legislative districts in the state of Tennessee came before the U.S. Supreme Court in the *Baker* case. Population shifts over time, along with the reluctance of the Tennessee legislature to redraw districts to conform to an equal population formula, resulted in terribly unbalanced and politically inequitable legislative districts across the state. However, rather than let judicial precedent set in *Colegrove* stand, the Supreme Court ruled that the issue of malapportioned legislative districts was justiciable. The issue, in the Court's view, involved the constitutional principle of equal protection under the law as guaranteed in the Fourteenth Amendment of the United States Constitution and thus belonged before the federal courts. As Robert B. McKay notes, "*Baker v. Carr* disposed of all the preliminary jurisdictional barriers which had earlier prevented Supreme Court determination of appropriate constitutional standards for state legislative apportionment."[41] With reapportionment now considered justiciable, the door had been opened to a broad variety of legal complaints involving inequitable legislative representation. In the years immediately following the Baker ruling, the Supreme Court issued a series of landmark judicial rulings that remain the law of the land to this day.

In *Gray v. Sanders*, 372 U.S. 368 (1963), which was not technically a legislative reapportionment case, the Court addressed the county unit system of nominating statewide officials in the state of Georgia. Rural dominance in statewide elections troubled the Court, and in striking down the Georgia plan the Court articulated the importance of the one person-one vote principle. Like *Baker*, the *Gray* case served as a foundation ruling for subsequent reapportionment decisions.[42]

The following year, in *Wesberry v. Sanders*, 376 U.S. 1 (1964), malapportioned congressional districts were ruled by the Court to be in violation of the Constitution. This ruling extended the one person-one vote principle to federal representation. In the same year, the Supreme Court, in *Reynolds v. Sims*, 377 U.S. 573 (1964), extended the one person-one vote principle to both chambers of the state legislature. The Reynolds case is often identified as a leading example of the Supreme Court's firm belief that every person's vote should be equal in power. According to the Court, states should make every effort to prevent discernible population variance from one legislative district to the next. Voting equality and equal representation depend on periodic legislative redistricting, and population figures must guide the final shape and configuration of legislative districts.

Also in 1964, a case concerning malapportioned legislative districts in Connecticut was heard in federal court. *Butterworth v. Dempsey*, 229 F. Supp 754 D. Conn. (1964), decided by a panel of three federal judges, further confirmed the position of the United States Supreme Court regarding the reapportionment issue. The panel ruled that any state legislative election in Connecticut would be considered legally invalid in the absence of a comprehensive redistricting plan coordinated and enacted by the Connecticut General Assembly. The *Butterworth* ruling was affirmed by the United States Supreme Court in *Pinney v. Butterworth*, 378 U.S. 564 (1964). The *Butterworth* ruling placed Connecticut's malapportioned legislative districts under the judicial microscope:

> That defendants . . . are enjoined from doing any act or taking any steps in furtherance of nominating or holding

elections of senators or representatives to the Senate or House of Representatives of the State of Connecticut, and said defendants are further enjoined from certifying or in any manner declaring that the results of any such nominations or elections are valid or that the legislature of the State of Connecticut is properly or legally constituted, unless all senators and representatives are nominated and elected to the Senate and House of Representatives of the State of Connecticut pursuant to a redistricting of the Senate and a reapportionment of the House to be effected promptly by the General Assembly so that the voting rights of plaintiffs in the choice of members of both houses as guaranteed by the equal protection clause of the Fourteenth Amendment of the United States Constitution will not be impaired.[43]

As one can see, the federal courts traveled quite far with respect to advancing the cause of political equality. In 1946, the Court's position was that the issue of legislative reapportionment was too political. In 1962, the Court ruled that legislative reapportionment was justiciable. In 1964, the Court issued a series of rulings requiring reapportionment in federal and state legislative districts. Judicial activism, not judicial restraint, was clearly the better approach to correcting the problem of grossly malapportioned legislative districts.

The rulings described above exerted direct influence upon national and state politics, Connecticut's included. The rulings of the Supreme Court, as noted earlier, were directly related to the call for a constitutional convention in Connecticut and the writing of an entirely new constitution in 1965. Connecticut's malapportioned legislative districts had been found to be in violation of the U.S. Constitution. However, instead of minor repair and political tinkering, the best remedy seemed to be political reform through the creation of a new state constitution. The new constitution was approved by Connecticut voters in a popular referendum on December 14, 1965, and formally proclaimed by the governor as the official and supreme body of law for the state of Connecticut on December 30 of the same year. Connecticut's current constitution consists of Fourteen Articles and, at the time of this writing, thirty Amendments.[44]

A State Constitution that Protects Rights and Liberties

Although the federal constitution over the years has served as a principal foundation for American civil liberties and civil rights, it is nevertheless imperative to emphasize the growing importance of state constitutions as documents that also preserve and protect the freedoms of the American people. Far too little is known about this fairly recent development in the field of constitutional law, yet it is one of the most fascinating developments within the context of American jurisprudence. The trend appears to have started in earnest with a seminal article published by U.S. Supreme Court Justice, William J. Brennan, in *The Harvard Law Review*, in January, 1977.[45] Brennan's article revolutionized the means by which civil liberties and rights would be protected.

After serving twenty years on the U.S. Supreme Court, Brennan had arrived at the conclusion that the federal courts had become deficient with respect to advancing the cause of civil liberties and civil rights. The conservative trend in federal judicial rulings, precipitated by the appointment of conservative judges to the federal bench during the six-year Nixon presidency, was a troubling development to Justice Brennan, who over the years had acquired a reputation as a liberal Justice. In response to judicial conservatism at the federal level, Brennan urged civil liberties and civil rights lawyers to argue their cases by utilizing provisions in state constitutions, rather than similar provisions in the federal constitution. State constitutions contain more rights compared to the federal constitution and state judges are allowed to interpret liberties contained in state constitutions above and beyond the federal standard. Moreover, state constitutional rulings cannot be appealed to the U.S. Supreme Court. In Justice Brennan's view, state constitutions would therefore afford more protection for American civil liberties than would the federal constitution.

Justice Brennan's law review article would serve as the chief catalyst behind a wide range of innovative, creative, and controversial state constitutional cases in years to come.[46] In Connecticut, the use of the state constitution to advance civil liberties and rights would result in a series of remarkable and very liberal state supreme court rulings. Such rulings would extend rights well beyond the federal standard. Equalized spending for public schools in suburban and urban school districts,[47] the use of Medicaid funds to pay for an indigent woman's abortion,[48] extended protection of the right to legal counsel,[49] additional safeguards against police searches and seizures,[50] as well as the controversial ruling that the state of Connecticut, not the local community, was constitutionally obligated to provide a quality and equal education to minority children who attended public school in the impoverished city of Hartford,[51] were among the several state supreme court rulings based on the state constitution that were reflective of Justice Brennan's revolutionary strategy for advancing civil liberties and civil rights.

This is not to suggest that the Connecticut supreme court is permanently embarked on a liberal path with regard to state constitutional interpretation. The tenure of a state supreme court judge in Connecticut is for eight years. Although judges can be reappointed, personalities on the court do change and the ideology of the court can potentially be transformed due to the outcome of gubernatorial elections. Nevertheless, despite changes in court personnel, one can be assured that Connecticut's constitution will continue to serve the needs of the state's citizenry well into the twenty-first century.

Notes

1. An excellent account of John Adams's pivotal role in writing the Massachusetts Constitution can be found in David McCullough, *John Adams* (New York: Simon and Schuster, 2001), pp. 220-25. Data regarding state constitutions, including the number of constitutions adopted by

states, date of adoption, number of words in state constitutions, as well as number of proposed and adopted amendments can be found in *The Book of the States* (Lexington: The Council on State Governments, 2004), 36:10.

2. Albert E. Van Dusen, *Puritans Against the Wilderness: Connecticut History to 1763* (Chester, CT: Pequot Press, 1975), pp. 28-29.

3. Quoted in the *Connecticut Register and Manual* (Hartford: State of Connecticut, 2000), p. 55.

4. Ellsworth S. Grant, *The Miracle of Connecticut*. (Hartford: Connecticut Historical Society, 1992), p. 20.

5. Vincent Wilson, Jr. *The Book of Great American Documents*, (Brookeville, MD: American History Research Associates, 1993), pp. 5-10.

6. Wilson, *The Book of Great American Documents*, p. 5.

7. Interview with R. Bryan Bademan, Assistant Professor of History, Sacred Heart University, June 16, 2006.

8. Van Dusen, *Puritans Against the Wilderness*, pp. 52-54

9. Christopher Collier, quoted in Grant's *The Miracle of Connecticut*, p. 26.

10. Richard J. Purcell, *Connecticut in Transition: 1775-1818* (Middletown, CT: Wesleyan University Press, 1963), p. 113.

11. Van Dusen, *Puritans Against the Wilderness*, p. 54.

12. W.H. Gocher, *Wadsworth or the Charter Oak* (Hartford: W.H. Gocher, 1904), p. 216.

13. Gocher, *Wadsworth or the Charter Oak*, pp. 281-333.

14. Van Dusen, *Puritans Against the Wilderness*, p. 71.

15. Edward R. Lambert, *History of the Colony of New Haven* (New Haven, CT: Hitchcock and Stafford, 1838), p. 21.

16. Lambert, *History of the Colony of New Haven*, p. 32.

17. Lambert, *History of the Colony of New Haven*, pp. 31-32

18. Lambert, *History of the Colony of New Haven*, p. 33.

19. Lambert, *History of the Colony of New Haven*, p. 38

20. Interview with Christopher Collier, July 5, 2000. For a full transcript of this lengthy interview, see Gary L. Rose, *Connecticut Government at the Millennium* (Fairfield, CT: Sacred Heart University Press, 2001), pp. 51-58.

21. Jarvis Means Morse, *A Neglected Period of Connecticut History 1818-1850* (New York: Octagon Books, 1978), p. 3.

22. Morse, *A Neglected Period of Connecticut History 1818-1850*, p. 5.

23. Morse, *A Neglected Period of Connecticut History 1818-1850*, p. 4.

24. Quoted in Purcell, *Connecticut in Transition*, p. x.

25. Interview with Christopher Collier, July 5, 2000.

26. David M. Roth and Freeman Meyer, *From Revolution to Constitution: Connecticut 1763 to 1818* (Chester, CT: Pequot Press, 1975), p. 89.

27. Roth and Meyer, *From Revolution to Constitution*, p. 20.

28. Roth and Meyer, *From Revolution to Constitution, p. 92.*

29. Richard Hofstadter, *The Idea of a Party System: The Rise of Legitimate Opposition in the United States, 1780-1840* (Berkeley and Los Angeles: University of California Press, 1969), p. 200.

30. Wesley W. Horton, *The Connecticut State Constitution: A Reference Guide* (Westport: Greenwood Press, 1993), p. 11.

31. Roth and Meyer, *From Revolution to Constitution*, pp. 63-65.

32. Horton, *The Connecticut State Constitution*, p. 14.

33. Horton, *The Connecticut State Constitution,* pp. 14-15.

34. Horton, *The Connecticut State Constitution*, p. 15.

35. Horton, *The Connecticut State Constitution*, p. 16.

36. Horton, *The Connecticut State Constitution,* p. 16.

37. Robert B. McKay, *Reapportionment: The Law and Politics of Representation* (New York: Simon and Schuster, 1965), pp. 46-47.

38. McKay, *Reapportionment*, pp. 55-56.

39. Louis Fisher,, *Constitutional Rights: Civil Rights and Civil Liberties* (New York: McGraw-Hill Publishing Co., 1990), p. 1239.

40. *Colegrove v. Green*, 328 U.S. 549 (1946), at 555-56.

41. McKay, *Reapportionment*, p. 79.

42. McKay, *Reapportionment,* pp. 86-87.

43. *Butterworth v. Dempsey*, 229 F. Supp 754 D. Conn. (1964), at 790-91.

44. For a thorough annotation of the Connecticut Constitution replete with case citations, see Horton, *The Connecticut State Constitution.*

45. William J. Brennan, Jr., "State Constitutions and the Protection of Individual Rights," *Harvard Law Review* 90 (January 1977): 489-504.

46. A concise discussion concerning the applicability of state constitutions for the protection and expansion of civil liberties can be found in John J. Harrigan and David C. Nice, *Politics and Policy in States and Communities* (New York: Pearson Education, Inc., 2006), pp. 30-32. An excellent review can also be found in Sue Davis and Taunya Lovell Banks, "State Constitutions, Freedom of Expression, and Search and Seizure: Prospects for State Court Reincarnation," *Publius: The Journal of Federalism*, 17 (winter 1987): 13-31.

47. *Horton v. Meskill,* 172 Conn. 615 (1977). An excellent journalistic account of the applicability of the Connecticut state Constitution with respect to protecting the rights and liberties of the Connecticut citizenry appeared in *The Hartford Courant,* 28 October 1990, pp. A1, A10.

48. *Doe v. Maher,* 515 A2d 134 Conn. Super. (1986).

49. *State of Connecticut v. Stoddard,* 206 Conn. 157 (1988).

50. *State of Connecticut v. Marsala,* 216 Conn. 150 (1990).

51. *Sheff v. O'Neill,* 238 Conn. 1 (1996).

CHAPTER THREE

How "Blue" is Connecticut?

Prior to the presidential election of 2000, the electoral maps used by the major networks during their election night coverage would designate states carried by Republican presidential candidates as blue, while those states in which the Democratic candidates won were colored red. Beginning with the election of 2000, the colors were inexplicably reversed, with states voting Republican designated as red and those voting for the Democratic ticket shaded in blue. It was also during the 2000 election that states began acquiring red and blue labels not only to portray a state's presidential voting pattern, but also to identify a state's ideological orientation. In addition to voting Republican for president, a red state was now considered a conservative state with a citizenry that was right of center. Blue states were where Democratic candidates would fare well, and where many liberal and left of center voters resided. "Red state" and "blue state" labels remained in place during the presidential election of 2004, and continue to be used by political pundits when analyzing voting patterns and political leanings among the fifty states. Indeed, red state and blue state labels have practically become an accepted part of the American political vocabulary. Such designations often mask the complexity of state politics, but in the world of sound bites and journalistic commentary the colors serve to simplify and organize political analysis.

The state of Connecticut, not long ago regarded as a swing state in presidential politics, is now described by political observers as a blue state. Connecticut is predicted to vote for the Democratic presidential ticket every four years and elect U.S. senators and members of Congress who are moderate to liberal in their political beliefs. Candidates for governor, as well as candidates for statewide constitutional offices, are advised to embrace moderate and liberal causes if they wish to have a political future in Connecticut, regardless of party affiliation. Although there are still some local communities in Connecticut that elect conservative Republican state lawmakers, such communities are relatively few in number. The state of Connecticut is now among those states in the Northeast, the upper Midwest, and the Pacific Rim that are designated "blue."

Two major bodies of evidence should be explored in order to document the political persuasion and ideological orientation of a particular state. Such evidence includes a range of election results, as well as public opinion among the state's voting age population. Although there is every reason to believe that Connecticut has become a more liberal state, it is still necessary to explore data that may, or may not, document this general characterization.

Presidential Election Results

Prior to the collapse of the stock market and the advent of the Great Depression in 1929, Connecticut was a very Republican state. As electoral college maps reveal, Connecticut supported Republican presidential candidates in fifteen of the twenty presidential contests from 1856, the first presidential election in which the Republican Party fielded a presidential candidate, through 1932. However, with the Republican Party and Republican President Herbert Hoover blamed for the nation's economic collapse, the country's political landscape, Connecticut included, underwent a major partisan realignment.[1] As a result of a dramatic shift in party allegiance among millions of voters, the Democratic Party under the leadership of Franklin D. Roosevelt thus became the nation's dominant party. In many states where the Democratic Party had been overshadowed by the Republican Party, the Democrats were able to eclipse the Republicans as the state's majority party, or at the very least compete with the Republicans on an equal basis.

In Connecticut, the new pattern that emerged during the Depression was one of vibrant two-party competition. From 1932 through 1960, Democratic and Republican presidential candidates were each able to win the state of Connecticut four times, a perfectly even split in the number of election victories.[2] Healthy two-party competition would continue in presidential elections over the course of the next thirty years. In the elections of 1960, 1964, and 1968, Connecticut voted for the presidential candidates of the Democratic Party. However, in the presidential elections of 1972, 1976, 1980, 1984, and 1988, Connecticut voted for the Republican presidential candidates. From 1960 through 1988, the Democrats carried the state of Connecticut in three presidential election contests, while the Republicans were victorious in five.

Several presidential contests in Connecticut between 1960 and 1988 were exceptionally competitive, while several were landslide elections. In the presidential election of 1960, Massachusetts Senator John F. Kennedy won 53.7 percent of the vote in Connecticut, while Richard M. Nixon, a former California senator and vice-president under President Dwight Eisenhower, won 46.3 percent of the vote, a 7.4 point margin of victory for the Democratic candidate. Both Kennedy and Nixon were regarded as centrist presidential candidates. The election of 1964 was a Democratic landslide. President Lyndon B. Johnson, a former Texas senator and vice-president under President Kennedy, and who succeeded to the presidency following Kennedy's assassination, secured 67.8 percent of the vote in Connecticut, compared to 32.1 percent won by conservative Arizona Republican Senator Barry Goldwater. This was an enormous 35.7 point margin of victory for the incumbent president. In 1968, Hubert Humphrey, a former Minnesota senator and vice-president under Johnson, won 49.5 percent of the vote in Connecticut, while Nixon won 44.3 percent, a somewhat narrow 5.2 point margin for the centrist Democrat. Third-party candidate George Wallace, a charismatic states' rights governor from Alabama who supported racial segregation, won 6.1

percent of the total vote in Connecticut in 1968. The election of
1972 recorded yet another landslide, with President Nixon winning
58.6 percent of the vote compared to South Dakota Senator George
McGovern's 40.1 percent, an 18.5 point margin between the two
candidates.[3] McGovern was regarded as one of the most liberal
presidential candidates ever to be nominated by the Democratic
Party. The election of 1976 was once again highly competitive.
President Gerald Ford, a moderate Republican, won 52 percent of
Connecticut's vote while Georgia Governor and moderate
Democrat Jimmy Carter won 47 percent, a slim 5 point margin for
the Republican candidate. The election of 1980 was nearly a
landslide in Connecticut with conservative Republican Ronald
Reagan, a former California governor, winning 48.2 percent of the
state's popular vote compared to 38.5 percent for the besieged
President Carter. This was a 9.7 percent margin of victory for
Reagan. Third-party candidate John Anderson, a moderate
Republican Congressman from Illinois, received 12.3 percent of
Connecticut's total vote in 1980. As in 1964 and 1972, the election
of 1984 was also a major landslide. President Reagan, running for
reelection, received 60.7 percent of the vote in Connecticut, while
liberal Democrat Walter Mondale, the former Senator from
Minnesota and vice president under President Carter, polled only
38.9 percent. Reagan's 21.8 percentage point margin of victory in
Connecticut exceeded that recorded for Nixon in 1972. Intense
two-party competition returned with the election of 1988. George
Bush, a moderately conservative Republican who had served two
terms as Reagan's vice president, garnered 51.9 percent of
Connecticut's vote compared to 46.9 percent for Massachusetts
Governor Michael Dukakis, a 5 point difference.[4] Like Mondale,
Dukakis was also considered one of the more liberal Democrats
during that point in time.

Beginning in 1992, the Connecticut electorate began voting for
Democratic presidential candidates on a routine and predictable
basis. In 1992, Arkansas governor Bill Clinton, considered one of
the most talented governors in the nation, received 42.2 percent of
the state's popular vote, while President George Bush received 35.7

percent of the vote, a 6.5 percent margin of victory. The mercurial and populist H. Ross Perot, running as a third-party candidate, won 21.5 percent of the vote, an extraordinary showing for a third-party presidential candidate. The election of 1992 would prove to be the last competitive presidential contest in Connecticut for quite some time.

In 1996, Connecticut voted overwhelmingly to reelect President Bill Clinton. President Clinton won 52.9 percent of the state's popular vote, while the conservative Kansas Senator Bob Dole secured only 34.6 percent. President Clinton's 18.3 point margin was practically identical to that of President Nixon's in 1972. Perot, running once again as a third-party candidate, received only 10 percent of the state's vote, less than half of what he received in the previous election.

In election year 2000, Al Gore, a former U.S. senator from Tennessee and vice president under President Clinton, won 55.9 percent of the vote in Connecticut. Gore's running mate was the U.S. Senator from Connecticut, Joe Lieberman. Conservative Texas Governor George W. Bush, who would win the presidency following an unprecedented U.S. Supreme Court ruling concerning a disputed recount in Florida, received only 38.4 percent of Connecticut's vote. Gore's 17.5 percentage point margin over Bush in Connecticut could be attributed not only to Lieberman's popularity with Connecticut voters, but also to the liberal drift of the state's population in recent years.

In 2004, Massachusetts Senator John Kerry, known for his liberal stance on multiple policy issues, won 54.3 percent of Connecticut's popular vote. President Bush, who would win his reelection bid, received 43.9 percent of the state's vote. Kerry's 10.4 percent landslide win over Bush was revealing with respect to Connecticut's political and ideological posture.[5]

As we examine the results for Connecticut, it is evident that of the four most recent presidential elections, only the election of 1992 resulted in less than a ten point margin of victory for the Democratic candidate. The 1996, 2000, and 2004 elections in Connecticut were Democratic landslides, with margins of 18.3,

17.5 and, 10.4 percentage points respectively. Three landslide Democratic victories in a row, two of which were overwhelming victories, suggest a state that has become exceptionally hospitable to Democratic presidential candidates.

Democratic presidential candidates have also done very well with little variation among the state's congressional districts. In 1992, Bill Clinton won congressional districts one, two, three, and six.[6] Congressional districts four and five were won by President Bush.[7] However, in the election of 1996, President Clinton won the most votes in each of Connecticut's six congressional districts. In the 2000 presidential election, Al Gore also carried every congressional district in Connecticut. In 2004, John Kerry, like Gore and Clinton before him, won every congressional district, which now numbered five.[8] In essence, every congressional district in Connecticut for the past three presidential contests could have been colored "blue."

Connecticut's Congressional Delegation

Heading into the 2006 congressional mid-term election, Connecticut's congressional delegation consisted of three Republicans and two Democrats. While this might seem odd in a state designated as blue, and one in which Democratic presidential candidates have been winning every congressional district, the fact of the matter is that Connecticut's congressional Republicans were a far cry from the ideologically conservative Republicans elected from the red states of the West and South. In the tradition of "Rockefeller Republicanism,"[9] the three congressional Republicans were for all intents and purposes moderate in their politics and policy pursuits. The moderate political center describes the political orientation of former Congresswoman Nancy L. Johnson of the fifth congressional district. Former Congressman Robert R. Simmons of the second congressional district was also described as a very moderate Republican. Congressman Christopher H. Shays of the fourth congressional district was and is more moderate than Johnson and Simmons. Shays is in fact frequently described as a "liberal" Republican. The moderate to liberal positions embraced by the three Republican members of Congress explain their electoral success.[10]

Ratings published by the Americans for Democratic Action (ADA), a liberal lobbying organization founded in 1947, reveal how moderate Connecticut's Republican congressional delegation was compared to their Republican counterparts in Congress. On a scale of 0-100, with 0 representing the most conservative rating and 100 the most liberal, ADA's average rating for Republicans in the U.S. Congress, which includes the House and Senate, is 12.[11] Clearly, the vast majority of Republicans in Congress vote in a conservative direction on legislative roll calls. A collective rating of 12 is also a reflection of the intense partisan polarization currently present in Congress. In contrast, however, Connecticut's Republican congressional delegation received an average ADA rating of 56. Congressman Simmons was rated 55, Congressman Shays 70, and Congresswoman Johnson 45. Very few Republicans in Congress received similar ratings. Indeed, Congressman Shays was rated as the most liberal of all House and Senate Republicans. The only Republicans with ratings of 45 or higher included Representative Michael Castle from Delaware (50), Representative James Leach from Iowa (55), Representative Mark Kirk from Illinois (45), the two Senators from Maine, Olympia Snowe (65) and Susan Collins (45), Representative Charles Bass from New Hampshire (45), Senator Arlen Specter from Pennsylvania (45), Rhode Island Senator Lincoln Chafee (55), and Representative Ronald Paul from Texas (50). The ADA ratings indicate that among the twelve most moderate Republicans in Congress, one-fourth are from the state of Connecticut.

With regard to the Democratic House and Senate members from Connecticut, the ADA ratings suggested that Christopher J. Dodd is one of the most liberal members of Congress with a score of 100. Senator Joseph Lieberman received an ADA rating of 75, which is certainly on the liberal side of the continuum, but considerably less liberal than the rating for the state's senior senator. Congresswoman Rosa L. DeLauro, who represents Connecticut's third congressional district, received an ADA rating of 100, an identical score to that of her mentor and former boss Senator Dodd.[12] Congressman John B. Larson, who represents Connecticut's first congressional district, also received a perfect liberal rating of 100. The ratings of Connecticut's Democratic House and Senate members further support the frequent assertion that Connecticut is a very blue state.

State Politics

Presidential election results and the ideological orientation of a state's congressional delegation are both useful indicators of a state's political leanings. Federal politics tend to involve a range of domestic and foreign policy issues that manifest themselves in value judgments on the part of the American people. The polarization of the American electorate in the twenty-first century and the current red state versus blue state dichotomy is a reflection of the highly contentious character of national rather than state politics. Nevertheless, in the United States politics is both a national and subnational affair, and to capture the political predisposition of a state one must also examine dimensions of political activity below the federal level. Gubernatorial and state legislative politics are useful for this purpose.

The Governorship

Connecticut's governors for the past fifty years, regardless of party stripe, have been moderate in their views and stances. Democratic governors Abraham Ribicoff (1955-61), John Dempsey (1961-71), Ella T. Grasso (1975-80), and William A. O'Neill (1980-91) were essentially moderate Democrats who governed without ideological agendas. They were Democrats in the traditional sense in that they favored a somewhat expanded role of government and looked to unions, urban areas, minority groups, and the working class for political support. Republican governors John Davis Lodge (1951-55), Thomas J. Meskill (1971-75), John G.

Rowland (1995-2004), and M. Jodi Rell (2004 to the present) drew their political support from the suburbs, wealthier voters, business interests, and the white-collar class. Nevertheless, Connecticut's Republican governors, in the tradition of Rockefeller Republicans, were also moderate in their approach to governance. Years of a state legislature under the control of the Democratic Party also encouraged Republican governors to embrace centrist and at times liberal causes. Even Governor Rowland, who had gained a reputation as a brashly conservative congressman, endorsed liberal positions on social and moral issues. His unparalleled support for urban renewal in several of Connecticut's cities was also surprising, given his Republican credentials.

As the state's Lieutenant Governor, M. Jodi Rell succeeded to the governorship following Governor Rowland's resignation from office, the end result of a scandal that consumed the Rowland administration and several close associates. During her tenure in office Governor Rell has enjoyed extraordinarily high public approval ratings, which have hovered between 75 and 80 percent. Governor Rell's support is also uniform across the eight counties of Connecticut and very high among Republicans, Democrats, and unaffiliated voters. She is also popular among both women and men.[13]

Although Governor Rell's unpretentious and down-to-earth persona is relevant to her approval ratings, it is really the governor's politics more than any other variable, including a healthy state economy during her tenure in office, that explains her broad base of popular support. Governor Rell, not surprisingly, supports positions that reflect the moderate to liberal character of the state's population. For example, Governor Rell supported legislation that allows for civil unions in Connecticut. Moreover, the Governor endorsed campaign finance reform, along with legislation that would expedite stem cell research. Support for civil unions, campaign finance reform, and stem-cell research are positions traditionally embraced by Democratic politicians, not Republicans. Governor Rell's support for such issues clearly coincides with the values of the Connecticut citizenry. The Governor is also pro-choice on the abortion issue. Governor Rell's popularity among the Connecticut citizenry was more than evident in the 2006 election. The Governor received 63 percent of the vote compared to 35 percent for Democratic challenger and Mayor of New Haven, John DeStefano.[14]

Prior to the Rowland/Rell Administration, Connecticut experienced one of the most liberal and free-thinking governors in modern times. Lowell P. Weicker, Jr. (1991-95), elected as a third-party candidate, embraced numerous liberal causes. In addition to his liberal stance on moral issues, Governor Weicker was an adamant supporter of public school desegregation in Connecticut, even to the point of urging a radical redrawing and merging of local urban and suburban school districts. It was also Weicker who engineered Connecticut's highly controversial personal income tax, a policy that led to a massive and quasi-violent public protest on the lawn of the state Capitol. Formerly a three term Republican Senator and well known for his "maverick" political style, Weicker's conduct as a United States senator and as Connecticut's governor personified in many ways the brand of moderate to liberal politics endorsed by a sizeable contingent of the Connecticut electorate. Weicker was the quintessential Rockefeller Republican.[15]

State Legislative Elections

State legislative elections provide additional proof of a state's political complexion. From 1967 to the present, the Democratic Party in Connecticut has enjoyed dominance over the state house of representatives. With the exception of 1973-74 and 1985-86, the Democrats have consecutively won a majority of seats in the lower house of the General Assembly. From 1987 to 2005, the Democrats on average have occupied 62 percent of the seats, a most comfortable margin of power. In the mid-term election of 2006, the Democrats increased their power in the state house by garnering 70 percent of the seats. To further complicate matters for the Republicans, shortly after the election, Republican state representative Diana Urban from North Stonington, who represents the forty-third legislative district, announced that she had decided to switch parties and join the Democratic caucus. Urban's defection increased the Democrats' share of seats in the house to 71 percent.

Democrats have also enjoyed control over the state senate, although the ratio of Democrats to Republicans has been much closer. Like their Republican colleagues in the state house, senate Republicans occupied a majority of seats in 1973-74 and again from 1985-86. The Republicans also held a majority of senate seats from 1995-96. However, from 1997 to the present, the Democratic Party has ruled the senate, with the ratio of Democrats to Republicans expanding during this time period. From 1997 through 2000, Democrats controlled 52 percent of the seats, while the Republicans occupied 48 percent. In raw numbers, this was only a two seat margin. From 2001 to 2004, however, the average percentage of Democratic seats grew to 56 percent, while in 2005-06, the percentage Democratic seats increased to 64 percent.[16] In the election of 2006, the Democrats won 67 percent of the senate seats. The 2006 election therefore resulted in a veto-proof Democratic majority in the Connecticut General Assembly, yet another indication of a state that has become very "blue."

It should also be noted that while there are safe legislative seats within both political parties, the evidence shows a distinct advantage for the Democratic Party in this regard. In the 2004 state legislative elections, 82 percent of seats in the state house of representatives were either uncontested by one of the major political parties, or won by a margin of 10 or more percentage points. Of those house seats in either the uncontested or "safe" category, 68 percent were held by the Democrats. The same pattern appeared in the 2004 state senate contests. Eighty percent of senate seats were either uncontested or won by margins of 10 or more points, and within this category of non-competitive seats, two-thirds were won by Democratic candidates.[17] Granted, state legislative elections are very localized election contests and normally not characterized by the "wedge issues" that dominate national politics. Nevertheless, Democratic and Republican candidates for the Connecticut state legislature disagree on issues, most notably taxing and spending priorities, and while the ideological orientation of Connecticut politics may not be fully gauged from the results of such localized contests, the data still shed light on the political leanings of the state's electorate.

Public Opinion in Connecticut

One of the very best measures of a state's political orientation involves the attitudes of its citizens towards social, political, and economic issues. Collectively, such attitudes comprise a state's "public opinion." Public opinion polls are the most common means of evaluating where the residents of a state stand on a range of policy issues. Public opinion polls are scientifically conducted and by using refined and time-tested methodologies they allow one to generalize about the orientations of a state's population from a relatively small but representative sample of adults. For the purpose of this inquiry, the polling results of the Quinnipiac University Poll should prove instructive.

Released on April 7, 2005, a Quinnipiac Poll based on a sample of 1,541 registered voters discovered that a majority of Connecticut residents were very tolerant with regard to the contentious issue of civil unions. Fifty-six percent of persons surveyed favored a law that would support same sex unions in the state of Connecticut. Thirty-seven percent of persons were opposed to such legislation. Connecticut residents, however, were found to be less tolerant towards gay marriage, with 53 percent of respondents opposed to a law that would establish this right. Forty-two percent of persons polled favored a law protecting gay marriage. On both issues, however, the residents of Connecticut were more liberal than the nation as a whole.[18]

With respect to the highly volatile and politically divisive issue of abortion, a Quinnipiac Poll released on May 2, 2006, discovered that 31 percent of Connecticut residents believed that abortion should be legal in "all cases," while 38 percent supported legalized abortion in "most cases." The two figures combined suggest that a very large majority (69 percent) of the state's adult population favor the right to abortion. Beyond support for abortion, 78 percent of persons polled also expressed support for a law that would require Connecticut hospitals, including those of a Catholic denomination, to provide victims of rape with emergency contraception. Support for legislation requiring emergency measures in hospitals was also evident across demographic groups. The poll discovered 69 percent of Republicans, 85 percent of Democrats, 79 percent of Independents, 75 percent of men, 81 percent of women, and 84 percent of Catholics in agreement with such a law.[19]

The public's attitude towards the war in Iraq and President George W. Bush's job performance are additional indicators of a state's political posture. In Connecticut, it should come as no surprise in light of the state's presidential voting pattern that a large majority of residents are both opposed to the war in Iraq and have serious doubts about the competency and judgment of President Bush. A Quinnipiac Poll released on June 8, 2006, found that 63 percent of respondents were of the opinion that the war in Iraq was the "wrong thing to do." This was an eleven point increase in the level of opposition to the war over the course of the past two years. Moreover, attitudes towards President Bush seemed closely related to attitudes towards the war. Seventy-two percent of persons polled stated that they disapproved of George W. Bush's performance as president.[20]

Public opinion polls leave little doubt that Connecticut's citizens are moderate to liberal in their political orientations.

The 2006 Congressional Mid-Term Election

Lieberman versus Lamont: The Historic Democratic Primary

Perhaps no other event in recent years demonstrates more convincingly how blue Connecticut has become than the August 8, 2006, Democratic primary election between incumbent U.S. Senator Joe Lieberman and challenger Ned Lamont. Lamont, a millionaire from Greenwich, who made his fortune in cable television contracts with colleges and universities, decided to challenge Lieberman, who was seeking his fourth term in office. The central issue in the primary campaign was clearly the war in Iraq. Lamont opposed the war and advocated an American withdrawal. Lieberman supported the war and favored continued American involvement until the Iraqi government could be stabilized, essentially the same position as that of President Bush.

In the very early stages of the campaign, it appeared that Lieberman faced little opposition from Lamont and was once again coasting to reelection. A Quinnipiac Poll released on May 2, 2006, showed Lieberman with 65 percent support among likely Democratic voters to Lamont's 19 percent.[21] At this point in time, Lamont had little name recognition and his campaign was in an embryonic stage.

The Lamont campaign eventually went on the offensive with very dynamic campaign ads featuring the candidate surrounded by energetic young voters enthusiastically endorsing his candidacy. Lamont depicted the war in Iraq as a misguided foreign policy venture in terms of lives lost, lives ruined, and billions of dollars squandered. Lamont's anti-war message resonated with voters. A Quinnipiac Poll among likely Democratic voters released on June 8 showed Lieberman's support at 55 percent compared to Lamont's 40 percent. The Lamont campaign was clearly gaining momentum. In an effort to reverse the tide of growing support for Lamont, Lieberman forcefully defended his eighteen years as a United States senator. He emphasized his experience, seniority, and impressive record of constituency service. Lieberman not only stressed his long record of public service as a state lawmaker, state attorney general, and his tenure in the Senate, but also his deep roots within the Democratic Party.

Sensing a possible loss to Lamont in the Democratic primary scheduled for August 8, Senator Lieberman began a petition drive that would allow him to run as a third-party candidate in the November election in the event he lost the primary. Connecticut election law required that a petition with the requisite number of signatures be presented to the Secretary of State's Office on August 9, one day after the primary election. Throughout his political career in Connecticut, Lieberman had received strong support among moderate Democrats, Republicans, and unaffiliated voters. Thus, in Lieberman's view, he could win the general election, despite a defeat in the Democratic primary.

By the middle of the summer, the primary campaign between Lieberman and Lamont had become the focus of national attention. Media commentators, political pundits, and columnists were describing the primary contest as a "referendum" on the war in Iraq. Some analysts went so far as to describe Connecticut's primary as a referendum on the Bush presidency, due to Lieberman's close association with the president. Supporters of Lamont were quick to remind voters of how President Bush embraced and kissed Joe Lieberman on the floor of the House of Representatives following the President's 2005 State of the Union Address. "Remember the Kiss," became one of the rallying cries of the Lamont campaign.

A spirited and combative televised debate on the evening of July 6 between the two Democrats further elevated the status of challenger Lamont. Although the political novice seemed outmatched at the start of the debate in terms of poise and substance, he quickly gained confidence and composure as the debate wore on. Much to the surprise of debate watchers, Lamont demonstrated a command over an array of domestic issues in addition to foreign policy. Although opposition to the Iraq war was the centerpiece of the Lamont campaign, it was now evident that the challenger was not a single-issue candidate. The debate served to bolster Lamont's bid for the Democratic Party's nomination. A Quinnipiac Poll released on July 20, 2006, showed Lamont at 51 percent among likely Democratic voters with Lieberman at 47 percent. The challenger had eclipsed the incumbent.

Following the debate, both campaigns went into overdrive. Both candidates feverishly crisscrossed the state, delivering speeches before large crowds and airing powerful campaign ads. Several ads, as expected, castigated the opponent in derisive terms. Both candidates engaged in negative campaigning. As the August 8 primary approached, it became evident that Lamont's campaign strategy and anti-war message had effectively mobilized many

Democratic voters. A Quinnipiac Poll released on August 3, only five days prior to the primary, showed Lamont with a commanding lead among likely Democratic voters, 54 percent to 41 percent. Some pundits suggested that a landslide primary victory for Lamont was a distinct possibility.

The 13 point lead, however, provided to be somewhat fleeting. On August 7, the day before the primary, a Quinnipiac Poll showed Lamont's lead cut to 6 points, 51 percent to 45 percent. It was evident that a portion of Democratic voters who might have initially turned against Lieberman were now reevaluating their support for the inexperienced challenger. Leading political personalities also appeared in Connecticut on behalf of both candidates during the final days of the primary campaign. President Clinton visited Connecticut to endorse Lieberman, while Jesse Jackson, Al Sharpton, and California Congresswoman Maxine Waters campaigned on behalf of Lamont. The primary election was intensely covered by all the major networks, especially MSNBC's Chris Matthews. Throughout the summer of 2006 the tiny state of Connecticut, with slightly more than three million residents, was the epicenter of American politics.

Ned Lamont won the August 8 primary with 52 percent of the vote to Lieberman's 48 percent. The Secretary of State's office reported voter turnout in the August primary at 43 percent of registered Democrats, an unprecedented level of participation in a primary election in Connecticut. Although the election was very close, the primary contest was nevertheless a momentous event and described as a major upset. A three-term incumbent Senator, who had run for President in 2004 and who had had been tabbed as the Democratic Party's vice-presidential running mate in 2000, was defeated in a primary election by a political neophyte. In American politics, such a development is almost without precedent. Ned Lamont's powerful anti-war message, which reflected the mood of the Democratic Party in Connecticut, combined with a masterful campaign meticulously directed by Lamont's campaign manager, Tom Swann, resulted in Lamont's stunning primary victory. It was a historic primary election with potentially national implications.

In a less than magnanimous concession speech, Senator
Lieberman congratulated Lamont on his primary victory, but
quickly added that the election results reflected political
polarization and the politics of the past. Comparing the Senate
contest to a sporting event, Lieberman stated that the Lamont
campaign had won the first half of the game, while the second half,
which was just now beginning, would be won by him. The Senator
announced that he would continue his campaign for reelection to
the U.S. Senate as an "Independent Democrat." The following day,
in compliance with state law, Lieberman's petition for a third-party
candidacy with the required number of signatures was filed with the
Secretary of State's Office. His "third party" was officially named
"Connecticut for Lieberman."

With respect to voting behavior within the primary election,
there appeared to be a very clear class division within the
Democratic Party. Lamont received a significant portion of his
support from young, well-educated, and liberal anti-war
Democrats, many of whom were located in the more affluent towns
of Connecticut. Liberal bloggers were also strong supporters of the
Lamont campaign, although it is difficult to determine if blogs such
as "My Left Nutmeg," "Firedog Lake," and the "DailyKos" merely
reinforced the views of young voters or actually structured political
orientations towards the two candidates. Several pundits have
suggested that the "blogosphere" propelled the Lamont candidacy,
although such generalizations need to be supported with additional
research. The appearance of Internet bloggers was first observed
during the 2004 presidential campaign of liberal Democrat and
former Vermont governor Howard Dean.

Senator Lieberman was supported in the primary by moderate
and older Democrats, organized labor, and urban voters. The
Connecticut chapter of the AFL-CIO had endorsed Lieberman at
its state convention, although the endorsement was for the primary
only, not the general election. Lieberman's close association with the
Bush administration explains why the unions issued a qualified
endorsement. Unlike Lamont's support among the affluent
Connecticut suburbs, Lieberman's principal base of support

appeared to be Connecticut's cities. Election results revealed that the only communities in Connecticut where Lieberman actually won the most votes were the five cities with populations of over 100,000. This included the cities of Hartford, Waterbury, New Haven, Bridgeport, and Norwich. The class division in the Democratic primary contest was acute.[22]

Following the Democratic primary, the race for the U.S. Senate was predicted to be very close. A post-primary Rasmussen Poll of 500 likely voters conducted during August 9-10 and released on August 12 showed Lieberman with a 5 point lead over Lamont, 46 percent to 41 percent. Alan Schlesinger, the Republican nominee, was supported by only 6 percent of likely voters. Schlesinger, a former state lawmaker and mayor of Derby, was never considered a viable candidate after it was learned that he had gambled at one of Connecticut's casinos under the alias Alan Gold. It was also revealed that Schlesinger was sued by a New Jersey casino over a gambling debt. Despite the Republican establishment's plea for Schlesinger to withdraw his candidacy, and despite the fact that President Bush refused to endorse his bid for office, the combative Schlesinger remained in the race.

The campaign themes of the three candidates were somewhat predictable. Senator Lieberman continued to stress his experience and emphasized his bipartisan approach to governing. The Senator presented himself as an experienced and practical consensus builder in an age of destructive party polarization. Ned Lamont continued to criticize the war in Iraq and the Bush administration's foreign policy. At the same time, Lamont attempted to expand his appeal beyond his Democratic base by discussing domestic issues, such as Social Security, education and job growth. Schlesinger, who performed remarkably well in the three debates, presented himself as the only true conservative in the race. Schlesinger tried to rally Republican voters on his behalf by depicting both Lieberman and Lamont as liberal Democrats.

On election day, Senator Lieberman prevailed in a fairly convincing fashion, thus winning a fourth consecutive term to the U.S. Senate. His strategy of forming a third party and running as an

"Independent Democrat" proved to be successful. The incumbent senator won 50 percent of the vote, while Lamont received 40 percent, thus leaving Schlesinger with a mere 10 percent.[23] Lieberman's emphasis on experience and his bipartisan approach resonated with voters across the political spectrum, particularly among Republicans and Independents. Exit polls indicated that 70 percent of Republican, 54 percent of Independent, and 33 percent of Democratic voters opted for Lieberman. Sixty-five percent of Democratic voters supported Lamont, along with 35 percent of Independents, and only 8 percent of Republicans. Lamont had limited success in expanding his base beyond the Democratic Party. Twenty-one percent of Republican voters supported Schlesinger, along with 10 percent of Independent and only 2 percent of Democratic voters.[24] Schlesinger appealed to a very small slice of conservative voters who chose to remain loyal to the Republican Party's official candidate. Although Senator Lieberman was and is a supporter of the ongoing war in Iraq, the 2006 U.S. senate election was in reality a contest between a very liberal Democrat (Lamont) and a moderately liberal Democrat (Lieberman); in essence a contest between two Democrats. The conservative Republican candidate Alan Schlesinger for all intents and purposes was a marginal presence in the campaign. Generally speaking, the Republican Party was barely noticeable.

The Five House Seats

The races for the five seats for the House of Representatives continue to document a steady and growing liberal pattern of politics in Connecticut. Two of the three moderate Republicans were defeated in their bid for reelection by liberal Democrats. In the fifth congressional district, Republican Congresswoman Nancy Johnson, who at the start of the campaign seemed certain to win reelection, lost to thirty-two year old Democratic state senator Christopher Murphy. These results were shocking. Murphy won 57 percent of the vote to Johnson's 43 percent, a landslide victory for the youthful Democrat.[25] Connecting Johnson to President Bush and emphasizing the Congresswoman's close association with special interest groups was at the core of Murphy's strategy. While such a strategy certainly contributed to Murphy's victory, the deciding factor, in this author's view, appeared to be Johnson's own distasteful, personal, and negative ads, which undoubtedly caused many voters to question her sense of ethics and fair play. Johnson's ads, which were orchestrated by the Republican Congressional Campaign Committee, resulted in Murphy winning the fifth congressional district. Congresswoman Johnson self-destructed in 2006.

Republican Congressman Rob Simmons in the second congressional district lost his seat to Democrat Joseph Courtney, a former state representative who had previously challenged Simmons in 2002. The election was the closest of all the House races in the United States, with Courtney winning 50.1 percent of the vote to Simmons' 49.9 percent. The legally required recount revealed several inaccurate tallies in the original results. However, after several days of carefully recounting ballots, Courtney was awarded the seat by a margin of 91 votes. The election in Connecticut's second congressional district lends further credence to the old adage that every person's vote truly matters. In 2006, Courtney's portrayal of Simmons as an ally of President Bush seemed to be the deciding factor. Like many House races across the land, the Democrats had successfully nationalized the contest for Connecticut's second congressional district.

The results in the fourth congressional district proved to be a surprise to many political pundits, for it was here that the Republican incumbent was deemed to be the most vulnerable compared to his counterparts in the fifth and second districts. Nevertheless, Republican Congressman Christopher Shays prevailed by winning 51 percent of the vote to Diane Farrell's 48 percent. Farrell, who had served as First Selectwoman of Westport, had also challenged Shays in 2004, losing that contest by only 4 percentage points. Throughout the campaign, Shays was deemed an endangered incumbent due to his unwavering support for the war in Iraq. Pundits speculated that Farrell's strategy of linking Shays to the war, and more generally the Bush administration, would result in the incumbent's political demise. Why Congressman Shays won reelection is difficult to precisely pinpoint, although several variables seemed relevant. In this author's view, the major reason why Shays was able to win reelection was due to his late summer announcement following his fourteenth fact finding trip to Iraq that he would entertain the possibility of timetables for a phased U.S. withdrawal from the war. His support for timetables suggested to swing voters that the Congressman was flexible and adaptable regarding his position on the Iraq war. This was key to his survival in the fourth congressional district.

Additional variables were also at work in this contest. The working class city of Bridgeport, a bastion of Democratic politics, failed to deliver a large vote for Farrell. The Democratic Party machine was less than enamored of the well-to-do former selectwoman from the wealthy town of Westport. Moreover, Shays, who is originally from Stamford, is now a homeowner and resident of Bridgeport. Although not a native of the city, the Congressman managed to forge important ties with the city's political establishment. One can also point to the favorable perceptions many voters have towards Chris Shays as a person. He is well-liked by his constituents and deemed by many to be an ethical and thoughtful public servant. One is hard pressed to find a person in the fourth congressional district who dislikes Chris Shays. Many people know the Congressman and respect him. Additionally, one needs to cite the Congressman's exceptionally effective staff located in the city of Bridgeport. For many years the Congressman's personal staff has met the needs of his constituents. Finally, Shays's strong support for campaign finance reform, which was at odds with his party's congressional leadership, further contributed to his support among reform-minded voters. Voters in the Fourth Congressional District appreciated Congressman Shays's "maverick spirit." Thus, a confluence of factors seemed to contribute to Congressman Shays's reelection victory. His reelection was surprising to many, but in retrospect it was an understandable outcome.

The two races in the first and third congressional districts were foregone conclusions and for the most part received very little media coverage. Both seats are extremely safe Democratic seats, with the results never in doubt. Congressman John Larson in the first congressional district won 75 percent of the vote compared to Republican challenger Scott MacLean's 25 percent. In the third congressional district, Congresswoman Rosa DeLauro won 76 percent of the vote, while the Republican challenger Joseph Vollano received only 22 percent. Republican congressional candidates are essentially sacrificial lambs in both districts with little possibility of staging an upset. The socio-economic and political demographics of both congressional districts and the popularity of both Larson and DeLauro among their constituents explain the overwhelming Democratic landslides.

The results of the 2006 federal and state elections should leave little doubt that Connecticut politics has become very favorable towards the Democratic Party. With some rare exceptions, such as Governor Rell and Congressman Shays, Connecticut is firmly in the Democratic column. Conservative and even moderate Republican office-holders are now a very distinct minority. Can the Republican Party stage a comeback? What will it take to revitalize the GOP? These are legitimate questions that face Republican Party strategists in the years ahead.

Notes

1. Two seminal works on election realignments in American politics are Walter Dean Burnham, *Critical Elections and the Mainsprings of American Politics* (New York: W.W. Norton and Co., 1970) and James L. Sundquist, *Dynamics of the Party System: Alignment and Realignment of Political Parties in the United States* (Washington: Brookings Institution, 1973).

2. Sarah M. Morehouse and Malcolm E. Jewell, "Connecticut," in Andrew Apleton and Daniel S. Ward, eds. *State Party Profiles: A 50-State Guide to Development, Organization and Resources* (Washington: Congressional Quarterly, 1997), p. 46.

3. Richard Scammon, ed., *America Votes: A Handbook of Contemporary Election Statistics,* volume 11 (Washington: Congressional Quarterly, 1975), pp. 7-13.

4. *Statement of Vote, 1976-1988* (Hartford: Office of Secretary of State).

5. *Statement of Vote, 1992-2004* (Hartford: Office of Secretary of State).

6. District one is in the central part of the state and includes the city of Hartford and surrounding communities. District two covers the eastern half of the state. New London, Norwich, and Storrs are communities in this district. District three is where the city of New Haven is located and covers other communities throughout New Haven County. District six, which no longer exists, due to reapportionment, was located in the northwest part of the state, with communities in Litchfield County and beyond contained within its borders.

7. District four is largely the Fairfield County district, which includes many wealthy communities such as Westport and Greenwich, but also the impoverished city of Bridgeport. The Fifth district, which eventually was merged with the sixth, included the city of Waterbury and extended westward to Danbury and the New York border.

8. *Statement of Vote, 1992-2004* (Hartford: Office of Secretary of State).

9. The term "Rockefeller Republican" is associated with the former governor of New York. Nelson Rockefeller represented the moderate wing of the Republican Party, which for all intents and purposes had been overtaken by conservative Republicans beginning with the Republican Party's nomination contest in 1964. Northeastern Republicans, such as those in New York and the New England states, including Connecticut, are known for their fiscal conservatism, yet liberal stance on social and moral issues. Such Republicans have become a distinct minority in a party now dominated by ideological conservatives from the South and West.

10. As of 2006, Simmons had served three terms in Congress, Shays ten terms, and Johnson twelve terms.

11. My figures in this section are drawn from Americans for Democratic Action, Ratings, 2004, online at www.adaction.org

12. Congresswoman DeLauro served as Senator Dodd's chief administrative assistant from 1981-86.

13. From August 19, 2004 to June 8, 2006, Governor Rell's public approval ratings have averaged 78 percent. In June of 2006, the Governor's approval rating among Republicans was 84 percent, 68 percent among Democrats, and 77 percent among Independents. Seventy-five percent of men and 76 percent of women approved of the way the Governor was

handling her job. Within the eight Connecticut counties, the Governor's approval rating was 77 percent in Fairfield County, 74 percent in Hartford County, 83 percent in Litchfield County, 76 percent in Middlesex and New Haven Counties, and 72 percent in Tolland, Windham, and New London Counties. Source: Quinnipiac University Poll, released on June 8, 2006, online at www.quinnipiac.edu/x11362.xml?ReleaseID=922.

14. Online at www.sots.ct.gov/ElectionsServices/election_results/ 2006_Nov_ Elections/ov.&%20LTGov/pdf.

15. Weicker's liberal political orientation and unique style of politics are thoroughly captured in his autobiography, Lowell P. Weicker, Jr., with Barry Sussman, *Maverick* (Boston: Little Brown and Co., 1995).

16. Online at www.sots.ctgov/RegisterManual/SectionIII/Leg3.htm. Political%20Division%200%20THE%20Connecticut.

17. *Statement of Vote 2004* (Hartford: Office of Secretary of State).

18. Quinnipiac Poll, released April 7, 2005, online at www.quinnipiac. edu/x11362.xml?ReleaseID=671. Commentary on Connecticut results in comparison to national opinion provided by Poll Director Douglas Schwartz.

19. Quinnipiac Poll, released May 2, 2006, online at www.quinnipiac. edu/x11362.xm1?ReleaseID=909.

20. Quinnipiac Poll, released June 8, 2006, online at www.quinnipiac. edu/x11362.xml?ReleaseID=922.

21. Quinnipiac tracking polls regarding the Lieberman/Lamont primary contest can be found at www.quinnipiac.edu/x1291.xml.

22. For a concise treatment of the class division within the Lieberman/Lamont primary that includes evidence of voting patterns, see Howard Reiter, "Connecticut Primaries Showed Class Divide Among Democrats," in *The Hartford Courant,* August 13, 2006, p. C6.

23. Online at www.sots.ct.gov/ElectionsServices/election_results/ 2006_Nov_Election/USSenate.pdf.

24. Online at www.msnbc.msn.com/id/14349736.

25. House election results are online at www.sots.ct.gov/ElectionsServices/ election_results/2006_Nov_Election/Congress.pdf.

CHAPTER FOUR

Mechanisms for Political Participation

For a democratic political system to function effectively, it is essential for citizens to have opportunities to participate in the political process. Thus, a government "for and by the people" requires political mechanisms that facilitate citizen involvement. The most effective way in which citizens can engage in and thus exert influence on the political process is by participating in elections, political parties, and interest groups. In this chapter, I explore each of these mechanisms.

Elections

Voting in elections is the most basic and least demanding means of participating in the political process. The opportunity to vote is one of the many freedoms enjoyed by the American people. Voting is a civil right that should never be taken for granted. Indeed, the existence of this right is what separates free countries from those under the yoke of totalitarian rule.

Like other states across the land, Connecticut politics is characterized by routine and frequent elections. During odd-numbered years, eligible voters can participate in local elections. Elections for a wide variety of local governmental posts occur in every one of Connecticut's 169 municipalities. Due to the home rule provision in the state constitution, towns and cities in Connecticut are allowed to create their own unique form of local government. Local government charters adopted by communities reflect the form of government that best serves the inhabitants of individual towns and cities. On occasion, a local community will adopt a new model of government in response to the town's changing economic, social, and political conditions. For example, the residents of Stratford in 2005 voted to change their local charter from a Council-Manager to a Council-Mayor form of government. Stratford now features a strong mayoral office with the mayor elected to a four year term.

In addition to electing mayors, councilors, or selectmen, local communities typically elect a variety of board members and commissioners. For example, local Boards of Education are elected in most Connecticut communities, along with Planning and Zoning Commissioners. Although town managers are appointed by town councils in several of Connecticut's communities, there is still no escaping the fact that local elected officials are the primary persons who structure and determine the quality of life in Connecticut's towns and cities. Elected local officials determine many policies, including mill rates, property taxes, school budgets, support for sports teams, additions to public schools, local school curricula, and community development. Local elections are critical events that directly affect a community's way of life.

During even-numbered years, the citizens of Connecticut have the opportunity to elect state and federal public officials. At the state level, candidates for the state house of representatives and state senate are directly elected by the people every two years. One hundred and fifty-one seats in the state house of representatives and thirty-six seats in the state senate are elected. As noted in the previous chapter, many of these seats, unfortunately, are either uncontested or non-competitive; this has become a troubling trend in Connecticut politics.

Every four years, the residents of Connecticut also elect the state governor and lieutenant governor, both of whom run on the same ticket. At the same time, several statewide public officials who occupy offices established in the state constitution are also elected. The "constitutional offices," as they are known, include the offices of attorney general, secretary of state, state treasurer, and state comptroller.

In addition to elections for state offices, federal elections for the U.S. House of Representatives, U.S. Senate, and the American Presidency will also take place during even-numbered years. Such elections are conducted coterminously with the state elections.

To vote in a general election in Connecticut, one must be a registered voter and a minimum of eighteen years of age. Registering to vote in Connecticut is a fairly simple process. Voter registration cards, readily available in government offices and public libraries, can be completed and mailed to the attention of the Registrar of Voters in one's hometown. Individuals can also register in person at their local town clerk's office, or download and complete a registration form from the Internet. Moreover, persons can register by completing the appropriate information on the form supplied by the Department of Motor Vehicles when applying for or renewing their driver's license. The latter registration process is the result of the National Voter Registration Act signed into law by President Clinton in 1993. The law, intended to stimulate voter turnout in the United States, was commonly referred to as the "Motor Voter Act." When registering as a voter, individuals can declare a party affiliation or select the unaffiliated category. Connecticut law requires that mailed registration forms be postmarked or received at an appropriate registration office at least fourteen days prior to an election. In-person registration must be completed at least seven days before election day.[1] Connecticut does not have "same day" or on-site voter registration.

Voter participation is more restricted in primary elections than in the general election. Despite calls to conduct "open primaries," in which unaffiliated voters would be allowed to vote, Connecticut's political parties continue to conduct "closed primaries." The decision to conduct open or closed primary elections was once determined by the state legislature. However, due to a U.S. Supreme Court ruling that emanated from Connecticut, the determination now belongs exclusively to the parties themselves.[2] In Connecticut, to be eligible to participate in a party's primary election a voter must be registered with the party. An individual who is registering as a voter for the first time, or who is registered as an unaffiliated voter and would like to register with a party for the purpose of voting in the party's primary, can register in person on the last business day before the party conducts its primary election. Thus, if the party's primary is on a Tuesday, which is likely, then a new voter or unaffiliated voter can register with the party as late as 12:00 noon on Monday, the day before the primary. If, however, a person wishes to switch party affiliation from Democrat to Republican, or Republican to Democrat, then he or she must register with the party at least three months prior to the party's primary election.[3]

Registration procedures in Connecticut, along with party nominating rules, have been criticized by political reformers for having a restrictive impact on voter participation. Reformers argue that little reason exists to require a specified time frame for voter registration prior to the day of the general election. Reformers have also urged state lawmakers to repeal the current registration law and legislate "same day" voter registration in Connecticut. Reformers also criticize the parties for conducting closed primaries, and recommend instead a system of open primaries in which all eligible voters irrespective of party allegiance are allowed to participate. As reported by the Office of Secretary of State on October 25, 2005, there were 699,502 registered Democrats (33%), 453,715 registered Republicans (22%), and 929,005 registered unaffiliated voters (44%) in the state of Connecticut. A total of 4,387 individuals (1%) were registered with minor political parties. Thus, over forty percent of Connecticut's electorate was disenfranchised during the 2006 nominating process, unless they chose, as 14,000 unaffiliated voters did, to register with a party prior to the primary. Thus, state laws and party rules will undoubtedly remain under much scrutiny at the state Capitol and in party circles in years to come.

It should be noted, however, that while political reformers advocate a more open and robust system of electoral politics in Connecticut, voter turnout in Connecticut is still somewhat respectable when compared to the national average. According to results published by the United States Elections Project, voter turnout in Connecticut among the eligible voting population in the 2004 presidential election was 65.2 percent, while the national average was recorded as 60.9 percent. Compared to other states, Connecticut ranks in the top 50 percent of states in terms of voter turnout, with only fifteen states recording higher levels of turnout in the 2004 election.[4]

Turnout in primary election contests in Connecticut varies depending on the nature of the nominating contest. Turnout in presidential primaries has not been impressive, with a mere 5.7 percent of Democrats voting in the March 2, 2004, presidential primary and 15 percent in the March 7, 2000, Democratic and Republican primaries.[5] The abysmal turnout in presidential primaries is more attributable to the competitive status of the presidential nominating contest in March than party rules or state election laws. For all intents and purposes the presidential nominating contest in recent elections had been decided by the time Connecticut conducted its presidential primary. Voters thus saw little reason to vote in a contest that was essentially over.

However, Connecticut voters will vote in very large numbers in primary contests when the campaign is contentious and the outcome uncertain. As noted in the previous chapter, on August 8, 2006, the Secretary of State's Office reported that 43 percent of registered Democrats voted in the Democratic primary that pitted challenger Ned Lamont against incumbent Senator Joe Lieberman for the Democratic Party's nomination for U.S. Senate.

It should also be noted that voting machines in Connecticut will soon be relegated to a historical footnote. In the Old Judiciary Room of the state Capitol on August 4, 2006, Secretary of State Susan Bysiewicz announced that beginning in 2006 and extending into 2007, voting machines in Connecticut will be replaced by an electronic optical scan voting system. The new system will feature scantron sheets similar to those used by students on standardized exams. After an extensive review of new voting systems and presentations by several companies, the Secretary of State's office selected LHS Associates from Massachusetts to receive the state contract. Additionally, beginning in 2007, more than 200,000 Connecticut residents with disabilities will be allowed to vote at the polling place with the assistance of a specially installed phone system. IVS, a company based in Louisville, Kentucky, received a one-year contract to provide this innovative service.

In order to evaluate the efficiency and accuracy of the new electronic system, the Secretary of State's office has entered into a partnership with the Department of Computer Science and Engineering at the University of Connecticut. The department's faculty served as consultants during the search for a new voting mechanism and concluded that security standards had been met to guard against hacking and manipulation of voting results. In a press release issued on August 4, 2006 by the Secretary of State's office, Secretary Bysiewicz was quoted as follows:

> Of all the concerns raised by citizens, academics, and advocates, security was No. 1. UConn has played an integral role in our decision-making up to this point. They have reviewed vendor proposals, tested equipment, and made recommendations for maintaining the highest level of security in our election process. We look forward to drawing upon their tremendous expertise as we move forward.

Connecticut's decision to adopt new technology for voting and to enfranchise the disabled complies with the "Help America Vote Act," a federal law imposed on states in the aftermath of the controversial 2000 presidential election. Although the new technology has been successfully field-tested in the towns of Windsor and Vernon, time will tell if the optical scan system and phone system for the disabled are in fact superior to conventional voting machines. An editorial in the *Hartford Courant* on August 14, 2006, regarding the new voting system was entitled "Dawn of a New Age in Voting." By 2007, the residents of Connecticut will know whether democracy has been enhanced by the implementation of new voting technology.

Political Parties

In addition to elections, political parties are also important and vital participatory mechanisms. Political parties are not mentioned in the United States Constitution and President George Washington warned the American people of the divisive impact of parties in his historic farewell address. Nevertheless, it was not long after the American republic was formed that the two-party system emerged. Although the names of parties and voter identification with parties have changed throughout the years, two-party competition has characterized American politics for over two hundred years. At the same time, it is more than evident that political parties, rather than corrode our country's politics, as President Washington suggested, have served to enhance and cultivate the quality of American democracy. In the oft-quoted words of E.E. Schattschneider:

> The rise of political parties is indubitably one of the principal distinguishing marks of modern government. The parties, in fact have played a major role as makers of government; more especially they have been makers of democratic government. Political parties created democracy and modern democracy is unthinkable save in terms of the parties.[6]

Although political party organizations and their respective leaders are nowhere near as powerful as they once were, the parties nevertheless still perform critical tasks essential to the functioning of a democratic system.[7] Moreover, for citizens who wish to participate in the political process, the political parties continue to provide a direct and convenient avenue for meaningful and immediate political participation. Thus, it is important to grasp the continued significance of parties, despite their diminished power.

Within the context of local, state, and national politics, political scientists have identified several critical electoral functions that are performed by political party organizations: political parties nominate candidates for public office; wage campaigns; and structure choice for the voting public at election time.[8]

The Nominating Process

Every election year, political parties are expected to nominate a slate of candidates. Whether it is a federal, state, or local election year, the parties present a team of Democratic and Republican candidates who are prepared to serve the public should they be elected in the general election.

Parties in Connecticut have a somewhat unique way of nominating candidates for public office. The nominating system, which has been in place since 1955, is a hybrid process that involves a nominating convention followed by the possibility of a primary election. In Connecticut, the primary is referred to as a "challenge primary." Connecticut was the last state in the country to adopt a primary election law and the primary system that was finally adopted was designed to dissuade candidates who did not have the support of the party organization from waging a primary contest.

The mechanics of Connecticut's hybrid nominating system are relatively simple. Delegates are selected to attend the party's nominating convention. If the candidates to be nominated are running for statewide office, such as the office of governor, lieutenant governor, attorney general, or the U.S. Senate, then the party will hold a statewide convention, normally in Hartford. The convention is run by the party's central committee and is presided over by the party's state chairperson. Democratic or Republican delegates from Connecticut's 169 local communities are chosen to attend the convention. If the candidates are running for a district-level office, such as U.S. Congress, state senate or state house of representatives, then smaller district based conventions will take place with delegates chosen to attend from towns within the district. In short, the process thus begins with a party convention. In most communities, delegates selected to attend the conventions are local town committee members along with local party activists. The delegates are often handpicked by local party chairs to attend the convention. If an individual who has not been selected by the town chair wishes to attend the convention as a delegate on behalf of a candidate, that individual has the right to wage a "delegate primary" within his or her party for the purpose of becoming a convention delegate.

At the nominating convention, a roll call will take place among the delegates. The candidate who wins the most votes at the convention is regarded as the "convention endorsed candidate." Candidates who do not receive the most votes at the convention, yet who receive a minimum of fifteen percent of the convention vote can, if they so desire, challenge the convention endorsed candidate in a primary election, hence the term "challenge primary."

It should be noted, however, that a recent reform significantly modified the challenge primary system in Connecticut. More specifically, a candidate who does not win 15 percent or more of the convention vote still has the option of challenging the convention endorsed candidate in a primary by petitioning his or her way onto the primary ballot. Thus, primaries can now occur in Connecticut due to the outcome of the convention vote, or through the petition process. The number of signatures required on petitions varies depending on the office that is being contested. State election law (Connecticut Public Act No. 03-241) requires a minimum of 2 percent of signatures among registered party members for statewide and congressional offices. A candidate for a statewide office, such as governor or U.S. senator, can collect signatures throughout the state, while a congressional candidate must collect signatures within the contested district. For the offices of state senator, state representative, and Judge of Probate, the threshold is 5 percent of registered party members, providing the districts are multi-town in scope.

Primary elections have been on the rise in Connecticut. Gone are the days when a powerful party leader could intervene in a nominating contest and dissuade a candidate from forcing a primary. Moreover, the 15 percent rule is hardly a difficult threshold for a candidate to overcome and the added option of petitioning one's way onto the ballot serves to encourage, rather than discourage, challenges to convention-endorsed candidates.

In 2006, primaries occurred for multiple offices in Connecticut, suggesting that the internal cohesion of the two major parties had become rather fractious. As discussed in the previous chapter, the most high profile primary occurred within the Democratic Party. Incumbent Senator Joseph Lieberman, seeking his fourth term of office, was challenged by Ned Lamont, a millionaire entrepreneur from Greenwich, Connecticut. The key issue in this primary was clearly the war in Iraq.

Two Democratic candidates for governor also faced one another in a primary contest. The mayor of New Haven, John DeStefano, Jr., and the mayor of Stamford, Dannel Malloy, engaged one another in a policy-centered campaign. Malloy had narrowly won a majority of delegates at the Democratic Party's nominating convention, yet lost to DeStefano in a close primary contest. Although the primary was between two successful, thoughtful;, and innovative mayors, the gubernatorial nominating contest received scant attention, due to the Lieberman versus Lamont primary contest. Moreover, it was well understood that regardless of which candidate the Democrat's ultimately nominated as their gubernatorial candidate, neither could defeat defeat the popular incumbent Republican governor, M. Jodi Rell, in the general election. Forecasts by political pundits proved to be correct, with Governor Rell winning well over 60 percent of the popular vote.

In addition to Democratic primaries for the U.S. senate and the governor's office, Democratic primaries were conducted for the position of lieutenant governor, ten state Assembly districts, two judges of probate districts, and in two towns for the registrar of voters. The Republican Party also held primaries in Congressional District One, and in two state Assembly districts. In total, twenty primary elections were conducted in election year 2006.[9] The increase in the number of primaries reflects the diminished role of party organization leaders in Connecticut with respect to structuring the outcome of the nominating process. The party's rank-and-file, rather than the party leadership, increasingly determines which candidates will represent the party in the general election.

The General Election Campaign

Following the nomination of candidates for public office, the parties in Connecticut move into campaign mode. All efforts are oriented towards winning the general election. However, with regard to the campaign function, it is evident that party organizations now supplement, rather than direct, the campaign efforts of the candidate's own organization. At one time, campaigns in Connecticut were organized, funded, and coordinated by the Democratic and Republican party organizations. Campaigns were very "party-centered." However, due to the rising cost of campaigns, as well as the increased availability of media as a voter mobilization tool, candidates at practically all levels of the state's political system began forming their own "candidate-centered" organizations and essentially waging their own campaigns.[10] Rather than resist such a development, the party organizations had little choice but to acquiesce in the new mode of campaigning. This is not to suggest that candidates for public office divorce themselves from their party during the election. Instead, there seems to be a mutual understanding between the party organization and their slate of candidates that the candidate, not the party, is primarily responsible for the management and coordination of the campaign. The party organization will, however, provide supplemental campaign services to candidates upon request.

According to Republican State Chairman George Gallo, the Republican State Central Committee in Connecticut provides an array of campaign services to Republican candidates, which in Gallo's words is similar to an "*a la carte*" menu.[11] Such services include assistance with fundraising, voter mobilization efforts, and consultation for effective messaging. In 2006, the efforts of the Republican State Central Committee were geared towards the gubernatorial and congressional elections, although Republican candidates for the General Assembly who were in closely contested races also received services from the State Central Committee.

Chairman Gallo also emphasized how modernized the Republican State Central Committee has become during the past several years. In particular, a sophisticated voter file has been developed and is routinely used by Republican candidates for voter mobilization purposes. The file precisely identifies the party registration of individuals in every one of Connecticut's 169 towns, and pinpoints who the likely voters are on election day. The file is exceptionally helpful to candidates for the purposes of targeting campaign messages prior to election day and for knowing which voters to contact and which voters to bypass.[12] Gallo mentioned that computer software and hardware at state headquarters have also been upgraded. Full-time staffing has increased as well. During the 2006 election year, the Republican State Central Committee was staffed by eight full-time employees. Following the election, the full-time staff was trimmed to five, including the chair, executive director, finance director, political director, and office manager.[13] Although Gallo fully acknowledged that party organizations no longer control the course of election campaigns in Connecticut, he did stress that the services provided to candidates still contribute to an important party presence within the context of Connecticut's electoral politics.

The Democratic Party in Connecticut has also modernized its state central headquarters, and appears to be providing similar "*a la carte*" services to Democratic candidates during election years. According to Nancy DiNardo, chairwoman of the Democratic State Central Committee in Connecticut, the voter file is clearly one of the most important services offered to candidates by the central committee.[14] She described the file as "state of the art" and frequently used by candidates at all levels of elections to identify their base of support as well as swing voters. Like the Republicans, the Democratic State Central Committee has a paid full-time staff consisting of six individuals who provide various services to candidates with fundraising strategies as well as the development of campaign websites. For some campaigns, the party will also provide money to candidates in need of additional assistance.

Like the Republican Chairman, Chairwoman DiNardo recognized that politics in Connecticut has become candidate-centered with the party organization primarily performing supplemental campaign services. Although the Democratic State Central Committee no longer controls the course of individual campaigns in Connecticut, in DiNardo's view the party organization still remains a valuable resource for Democratic candidates.

Choice at Election Time

In theory, political party organizations should also provide voters with a set of distinct choices at election time. The party label affixed to candidates should represent a particular philosophy of government. Theoretically, when voters enter the voting booth the party label should denote whether or not candidates are conservative or liberal on an array of policy matters. Moreover, once elected, parties should enact a coherent set of public policies. This is how political parties should govern according to the "doctrine of responsible parties."[15] Party platforms at one time served to structure the choices voters made between Democratic and Republican candidates. While state and national platforms are still issued by the parties, most people are quite unfamiliar with the contents of such platforms.

In Connecticut, platforms are occasionally issued by parties, but such documents tend to remain obscure. If platforms are issued, very few individuals ever lay eyes on them. Candidates, as noted above, are largely on their own with regard to campaign strategy and candidate platforms clearly supersede the party platform at election time. If voters feel there is significant ideological choice at election time, this is due to the positions articulated by the individual candidates in their own campaign literature, which is tantamount to a platform, rather than broad philosophical statements crafted by the party organization. Quite frankly, due to the moderate to liberal leaning of the Connecticut electorate, one is hard pressed to find any real evidence of an ideological chasm between the two major parties. The differences that do exist seem to concern taxing and spending priorities. However, on social and moral issues, the two major parties in Connecticut are largely in agreement. Compared to party politics at the national level, Connecticut's two-party system is less ideologically and politically polarized.

Interest Groups

Involvement with interest groups is yet another means through which citizens in Connecticut can participate in politics. For those individuals who wish to promote a specific cause, or set of causes, joining an interest group should prove to be a satisfying experience. Interest groups have become particularly important as political parties have receded in influence. As Burdett A. Loomis and Allan J. Cigler put it, "The weakness of political parties has helped to create a vacuum in electoral politics since 1960, and in recent years interest groups have aggressively moved to fill it."[16] Although this quotation appeared in a volume published in 1983, the notion of a "vacuum" resulting from party decline is perhaps even more relevant in 2006.

Interest groups in Connecticut, as well as in other states, can be categorized as either "special interest groups" or "public interest groups."[17] Special interest groups exist to promote the interests of a specific group or class of people, or perhaps a specific cause. The Connecticut chapter of the AFL-CIO (American Federation of Labor–Congress of Industrial Organizations) is a prime example of a special interest group that has been operating for many years in Connecticut politics. This is the umbrella organization that represents the interests of specific labor unions. Several large labor organizations are members of the AFL-CIO, including the American Federation of State and County Municipal Employees (AFSCME), the Firefighters Union, the American Federation of Teachers, the United Food and Commercial Workers Union, the International Association of Machinists, and several building trade unions, such as the Carpenters' Union. In total, the AFL-CIO represents approximately 210,000 union workers within the state of Connecticut.[18] The AFL-CIO has a clearly defined legislative agenda aimed at protecting the economic rights and living standards of the working class. In 2006, the organization's agenda at the Connecticut state Capitol included the preservation of statutes that protect binding arbitration, preventing corporate attempts to shift the cost of health care insurance onto workers, opposing job outsourcing, and protecting retiree benefits.[19] The Connecticut chapter of the AFL-CIO, like the national organization, is closely allied with the Democratic Party. In 2006, delegates to the AFL-CIO's state convention endorsed Democratic candidate John DeStefano for governor, and offered a lukewarm endorsement for incumbent Senator Joseph Lieberman.

Business interests are also well represented at the Connecticut state Capitol. Like the AFL-CIO, business interest groups have a clearly defined set of legislative priorities. Several organizations representing a broad array of business interests are a discernible presence at the Connecticut state Capitol.

One example of a business organization with a defined legislative agenda is the Chamber of Commerce. There is no state umbrella organization for the Chamber of Commerce in Connecticut. Instead, towns and cities have their own local chambers and, if needed, their own director of government affairs.

The New Haven Chamber of Commerce, for example, represents over nineteen hundred businesses throughout New Haven County. The businesses range from very large enterprises, such as Yale New Haven Hospital and AT&T, to small business operations, such as Allied Health Rehabilitation and Hula Hanks Restaurant in New Haven. Most of the activity of the New Haven Chamber of Commerce in 2006 was aimed at defeating legislation that was unfriendly towards business, rather than proposing new laws that favored business activity. For example, the Chamber opposed legislation that would restrict employers from conducting staff meetings with their employees to discuss matters of politics and religion. Such meetings are known as "captive audience meetings." The Chamber also opposed "pay or play" legislation that would impose a tax on businesses with a certain number of employees if the businesses were not providing their employees with health care coverage. The Chamber also opposed "neutrality agreements," which would ban employers of businesses that receive state financial assistance from discussing the effects of unionization on their companies with employees. Legislative restrictions on eminent domain for the purpose of commercial development were also opposed by the Chamber of Commerce.[20] The Chamber of Commerce generally supports Republican candidates at election time.

Apart from special interest groups that represent economic interests, such as the AFL-CIO and the Chamber of Commerce, there are a plethora of interest groups currently in Connecticut that exist for the purpose of protecting very specific causes. Special interest groups with very narrow agendas are commonly known as "single issue interest groups." Examples in Connecticut include the Connecticut Motorcycle Riders Association, the Connecticut Coalition Against Domestic Violence, Planned Parenthood of Connecticut, Friends of Animals, and the Marijuana Policy Project.

In addition to special interest groups, one also finds an array of "public interest groups" attempting to influence the state policy process. Public interest groups are organized to serve the public's interest, rather than a particular segment of society. Organizations concerned with environmental or consumer protection, as well as those organizations that seek to improve the quality of democracy in America, can be classified as public interest groups. Examples of public interest groups that are active at the Connecticut state Capitol include Common Cause, The League of Women Voters, Environmental Defense, and End Hunger. Data generated from the State Ethics Commission reveal that well over 700 organizations were present at the Connecticut state Capitol in 2003-04 for the purpose of influencing the lawmaking process.

Lobbyists

In order to exert influence over the state lawmaking process, most interest groups hire lobbyists and, if possible, contribute money to election campaigns. The term "lobbying," according to most accounts, originated under the presidency of Ulysses S. Grant. President Grant, at his wife's insistence, would smoke his cigars in the Willard Hotel lobby, rather than in the White House. While at the hotel, Grant would meet with individuals who would often seek to influence his position on issues and obtain favors from the President. Individuals who met with President Grant at the hotel thus became known as "lobbyists."[21]

Lobbyists can be classified under two categories: "client lobbyist" and "contract lobbyist." The client lobbyist is an individual who is an employee of one organization and is designated as the organization's lobbyist. The individual therefore lobbies exclusively on behalf of his or her client organization and is paid a salary by the organization. The individual is essentially an "in-house" lobbyist.

The contract lobbyist is an individual who operates a lobbying consulting firm and who lobbies on behalf of several organizations for a set fee.[22] The contract lobbyist is not an employee of the organization, but instead provides lobbying services on a contractual basis. Based on reports, it appears that most contract lobbyists charge their clients an annual, monthly, or retainer fee. In Connecticut, the consulting firms of Betty Gallo and Co., DePino Associates LLC., and Sullivan and LeShane are leading examples of active, well-connected, and very prosperous lobbying consulting firms. State Ethics Commission data report that Betty Gallo and Co. represented twenty organizations, DePino Associates, LLC. eighteen organizations, and Sullivan and LeShane thirty-eight organizations during the two year period of 2003-04. A review of registered lobbyists, or "communicators," as they are technically known, suggests that contract lobbying firms are proliferating at the Connecticut state Capitol. Moreover, lobbying in Connecticut and in other states has become an exceptionally lucrative business. According to a 2004 report issued by the Center for Public Integrity, of the forty-two states that reported lobbying expenditures, Connecticut ranks eighth in the nation with regard to fees and salaries paid to lobbyists. The Center reported a figure of

$27,161,810 paid to Connecticut lobbyists. California ranks first in the nation with lobbying fees and salaries reported at $212,695,872.[23]

Lobbying a lawmaker is a fine art that requires excellent personal and communication skills. The successful lobbyist is one who knows how to present facts in a succinct and well-organized fashion, without being overbearing, deceitful, or in any way threatening. Careful preparation is essential to effective lobbying. What lawmakers value most from a lobbyist is reliable information that will assist them in casting an intelligent vote on proposed legislation. Generating reliable and of course persuasive information is one of the key ingredients for a successful lobbying effort. Moreover, the successful lobbyist must know how to forge political coalitions on a particular issue, and he or she must understand the art of compromise.[24] In the words of Louise DiCocco-Beauton, a lobbyist for the Greater New Haven Chamber of Commerce, effective lobbying at the Connecticut state Capitol requires "identifying, analyzing, and in some cases, researching the impact pending legislation will have on various business organizations, and successfully communicating your position to legislators to secure passage or defeat of legislation."[25]

At the Connecticut state Capitol, lobbyists can be found discussing pending legislation with lawmakers outside the house and senate chambers, in the offices of lawmakers, in the atrium or cafeteria of the Legislative Office Building, and in the committee rooms where they frequently provide testimony on bills. It is not at all difficult to identify who the lobbyists are at the state Capitol, as the state ethics law requires all registered lobbyists to wear a badge that clearly identifies them as such. Outside of the state Capitol, lobbyists working on behalf of interest groups might also organize a public relations campaign on behalf of a public policy issue. State residents might be encouraged through direct mail or other forms of advertising to phone or e-mail lawmakers in order to influence the outcome of a bill before the legislature. Political scientists refer to this strategy as "grassroots lobbying."

While many associate the term "lobbyist" with behind-the-scenes legislative deals, secretive negotiations, and perhaps political corruption, the fact of the matter is that lobbyists perform a vital role within the context of the lawmaking process. State Senator Bill Finch offers this perspective:

> I can't imagine how the legislative process would work without professional advocates for the various points of view. The legislature deliberates, in a general way, like a court, in that information is provided by opposing interests to help reach a decision. The legislative process is much more informal and rough and tumble than a court, but nonetheless we have to process a lot of information, separating fact from fiction, and we need help. Special interests from oil companies and insurance companies to birdwatchers and child advocates all have lobbyists at the Capitol. It is important to remember who is paying the advocate and be up front with them about their interest in the outcome.[26]

Campaign Contributions

Campaign contributions are another method by which interest groups attempt to influence the Connecticut lawmaking process. Interest group money, individual contributions, the candidate's own money, and party money, all help to finance Connecticut election campaigns.

Contrary to popular belief, campaign contributions from interest groups do not determine a lawmaker's views on legislation.[27] Instead, campaign contributions appear to facilitate a group's access to elected officials. If an elected official, either in the legislative or executive branch, receives a campaign contribution from an interest group, it is well understood that the group is at least entitled to an audience with the official at some point in the future. Access, rather than manipulation, appears to be the end result of a campaign contribution from a special or public interest group.[28]

Similar to federal politics, interest group money in Connecticut election campaigns has become quite substantial. A significant portion of interest group money has been funneled to legislative, gubernatorial, and constitutional office candidates by both lobbyists and Political Action Committees.

Political Action Committees are either connected to organizations and serve as their political fundraising arms, or operate as freestanding committees not connected to any specific organization. An example of a "connected" PAC would be the one operated by the American Telephone and Telegraph (AT&T) Company. Freestanding or "nonconnected" PACs tend to be those with single issue or ideological agendas.[29] Nonconnected PACs are essentially a group of like-minded people who feel very strongly about an issue or cause and have formed a PAC for the purpose of promoting a clearly defined goal. Connecticut's N.O.W. (National Organization for Women) PAC would be one such example.

Also present in Connecticut are PACs that are under the control of political parties within the state legislature, known as "caucus PACS." There are also Legislative Leadership PACs (LLPs) that are directed by the party's legislative leaders. Such PACs are not to be confused with interest group PACs operating outside of the General Assembly. In total, there were more than 700 PACs registered with the Secretary of State's Office in 2006.[30]

Similar to the federal level, and other states across the land, PAC contributions in Connecticut tend to be directed towards incumbents, rather than challengers. As Alan Rosenthal notes, "Given their high reelection rates, incumbents are most likely to win, so they are the best bets for access-motivated giving."[31] Legislative leaders and committee chairs are often the main recipients of PAC contributions.

There are exceptions to the rule in every state legislative election. Take for example the 2006 state legislative campaign waged by Republican challenger Christopher DeSanctis. DeSanctis, challenged one term Democratic incumbent Tom Drew for the 132nd General Assembly district located in the town of Fairfield. DeSanctis raised $19,000 by the beginning of August and was among the top fundraisers for state legislative candidates. DeSanctis received contributions from a variety of supporters, including personal donations and legislative PACs. The fact that the 132nd district was regarded as a "swing" district, and Representative Drew was perceived as a vulnerable incumbent, encouraged donors to direct campaign dollars to the DeSanctis campaign. Commenting on his extraordinary fundraising success, DeSanctis put it this way:

> Fundraising is just a matter of asking. We all have friends and relatives that need to be solicited. The bottom line is no one wakes up in the morning saying to themselves, 'I have to donate to this or that campaign.' They need to be continually reminded until they give or say no."[32]

However, despite DeSanctis's extraordinary success at fundraising, as well as his energetic grassroots campaign, the power of incumbency proved too much for the challenger. Drew received 61 percent of the vote while DeSanctis won 39 percent.[33]

It is difficult to determine precisely the percentage of special interest money present in Connecticut politics *vis-à-vis* other forms of political money, and it is well beyond the scope of this work to describe the details of Connecticut's campaign finance code. Nevertheless, it is clear that interest group money has become an important element in Connecticut election campaigns and contributions to office holders have, at the very least, facilitated access to the corridors of power at the Connecticut state Capitol. Precisely what will become of special interest money is difficult to gauge and fully assess at this point in time.

The corruption and scandals that enveloped Connecticut politics, particularly the administration of Governor John G. Rowland, which resulted in Rowland's resignation and imprisonment, served as the catalyst for lobbying reform.[34] Investigations into Rowland's association with the Tomasso Construction Company revealed how ingrained special interests and contractors had become at the state Capitol. In 2005, a sweeping campaign finance reform law was passed by the

Connecticut General Assembly and signed into law by Governor Rell. The new law provides for public funding of statewide and legislative campaigns and severely restricts the role of lobbyists and contractors with respect to campaign contributions. The new law went into effect in 2007. As with most campaign finance codes, loopholes will inevitably be found and exploited that will lead to additional calls for reform.

Notes

1. League of Women Voters of Connecticut Education Fund, "A Guide to Voter Registration and Election Procedures in Connecticut," online at www.1w.vct.org.

2. This is the result of the landmark U.S. Supreme Court ruling, *Tashjian v. Republican Party of Connecticut* 479 U.S. 208 (1986).

3. League of Women Voters of Connecticut Education Fund, "A Guide to Voter Registration and Election Procedures in Connecticut," online at www.1w.vct.org.

4. United States Elections Project, "2004 Voting-Age and Voting-Eligible Population Estimates and Voter Turnout," online at elections.gmu.edu/Voter_Turnout_2004_Primaries.htm. The figures presented are based on the voting eligible population (VEP) rather than the voting age population (VAP). Unlike the VAP, the VEP only includes persons eighteen years of age or older who are legally eligible to vote. It does not include persons eighteen years of age or older who are ineligible to vote due to criminal records or citizenship issues.

5. United States Elections Project, "2004 Presidential Primary Turnout Rates," online at elections.gmu.edu?Voter_Turnout_2004_Primaries.htm

6. E.E. Schattschnieder, *Party Government* (New York: Holt, Rinehart and Winston, 1942), p. 1.

7. See Joseph I. Lieberman, *The Power Broker* (Boston: Houghton and Mifflin, 1966) and *The Legacy* (Hartford: Spoonwood Press, 1981), p. 213. Both of Lieberman's works focus on John Bailey, the legendary Democratic Party boss in the state of Connecticut. Both works provide rich insight into the influence and power wielded by party organization leaders in a previous political era.

8. Several works explore the broad functions of political party organizations. See, for example, William J. Crotty, ed., *Approaches to Party Organization* (Boston: Allyn and Bacon, 1968); and William E. Wright, ed., *A Comparative Study of Party Organization* (Columbus: Charles E. Merrill Publishing Co., 1971).

9. Data obtained from the Office of the Secretary of State website, www.sots.ct.gov.

10. The role of media in fostering candidate-centered campaigns is discussed in many works on political parties. For a succinct treatment, see Barbara G. Salmore and Stephen A. Salmore, *Candidates, Parties, and Campaigns: Electoral Politics in America* (Washington: Congressional Quarterly, 1989), chapter 3.

11. Phone interview with George Gallo, chairman of the Connecticut Republican State Central Committee, July 27, 2006.

12. Gallo interview. July 27, 2006

13. Gallo interview, July 27, 2006.

14. Phone interview with Nancy DiNardo, chairwoman of the Connecticut Democratic State Central Committee, August 15, 2006.

15. This is the perspective advocated by the Committee on Political Parties, *Toward a More Responsible Two-Party System* (New York: Rinehart and Co., 1950).

16. Burdett A. Loomis and Allan J. Ciglar, "Introduction: The Changing Nature of Interest Group Politics," in Allan J. Ciglar and Burdett A. Loomis, eds., *Interest Group Politics* (Washington: Congressional Quarterly Press, 1983), p. 20.

17. For a review of interest group activity and group categories, see Norman Ornstein and Shirley Elder, *Interest Groups, Lobbying and Policymaking* (Washington: Congressional Quarterly Press, 1978), pp. 35-53. A discussion of public interest groups can be found in Andrew S. McFarland, *Public Interest Lobbies: Decision Making on Energy* (Washington: American Enterprise Institute, 1976), pp. 1-43.

18. Data on membership obtained from phone call to central headquarters in Rocky Hill, Connecticut, July 31, 2006.

19. Connecticut AFL-CIO 2006 Legislative Agenda, online at www.ctaflcio.org.

20. My thanks to Louise DiCocco-Beauton, for supplying this information. DiCocco-Beauton is the Director of Governmental Affairs and lobbyist for the Greater New Haven Chamber of Commerce.

21. The origin of the term "lobbying" is often attributed to Grant's experience with individuals at the hotel who attempted to exert influence over his perspective on issues. See Jennifer Barrios, "Early Lobbyists Found 'in' Crowd at Willard Hotel," American Society of Newspaper Editors, April 22, 2004; online at www.asne.org/index.cfm?id=5217.

22. An informative overview of client and contract lobbying can be found in my lengthy personal interview with contract lobbyist Paddi LeShane. See Gary L. Rose, *Connecticut Government at the Millennium* (Fairfield, CT: Sacred Heart University Press, 2001), pp. 167-72.

23. Neil Gordon, "State Lobbyists Near the $1 Billion Mark," The Center for Public Integrity, August 10, 2005; online at www.publicintegrity.org/hiredguns/report.aspx?aid+728.

24. An excellent overview of what constitutes appropriate lobbying conduct and skillful strategizing can be found in Bruce C. Wolpe and Bertram J. Levine, *Lobbying Congress: How the System Works*, 2nd ed. (Washington: Congressional Quarterly Press, 1996), pp. 13-47.

25. Interview with Louise DiCocco-Beauton, August 2, 2006.

26. Interview with State Senator Bill Finch, September 1, 2006.

27. John R. Wright, "Tobacco Industry PACs and the Nation's Health: A Second Opinion," in Paul S. Herrnson, Ronald G. Shaiko, and Clyde Wilcox, eds., *The Interest Group Connection: Electioneering, Lobbying and Policymaking in Washington* (Chatham, NJ: Chatham House Publisher, 1998), pp. 174-95.

28. David Lowery and Holly Brasher, *Organized Interests and American Government* (Boston: McGraw Hill, 2004), p. 133; Alan Rosenthal, *The Third House: Lobbyists and Lobbying in the States*, 2nd ed. (Washington: Congressional Quarterly Press, 2001), p. 120.

29. Gary C. Jacobson, *The Politics of Congressional Elections*, 6th ed. (New York: Pearson Education, Inc. 2004), p. 73.

30. Online at www.sots.ct.gov/ElectionsServices/CampaignFinance/PACList1.Doc

31. Rosenthal, *The Third House*, p. 133.

32. Interview with Christopher DeSanctis, August 15, 2006.

33. Voting statistics available online at www.sots.ct.gov/RegisterManual/SectionVIII/SOV06Assembly.htm.

34. For a more thorough treatment of recent political scandals involving Connecticut public officials, see Gary L. Rose, ed., *Public Policy in Connecticut: Challenges and Perspectives* (Fairfield, CT: Sacred Heart University Press, 2005), especially Gary L. Rose, "Introduction," pp. 15-23, and Brian Stiltner, "The Challenge of Ethical Political Leadership," pp. 101-18.

CHAPTER FIVE

The State Legislature

The Connecticut Constitution of 1818, regarded as a critical turning point in the history of Connecticut's rich constitutional tradition, established a three-branch system of state government. Each branch of government was given its own independent sphere of constitutional authority and each branch was empowered to impose checks on the others. The separation of powers doctrine, combined with a system of checks and balances, was firmly embraced and maintained in the Constitution of 1965. Beginning with the devolution of power to state governments in the early 1980s and extending to the present, the three branches of government have been dramatically modernized to accommodate the growing needs of Connecticut's diverse population. Connecticut's residents currently expect a high level of performance from their state government, and rather than ignore and dismiss such expectations, the three branches of government have responded by modernizing their operations in practically every respect.[1] The end result is a state government with more capacity and hence more ability to effectively meet the changing and growing needs of the state's population. The modernization of the Connecticut state legislature will be the focus of this chapter.

The Connecticut State Legislature

Although still a part-time legislature, the Connecticut General Assembly in many ways exhibits the same characteristics as those of the United States Congress. This can be observed in the extraordinary structural changes that have taken place at the state Capitol during the 1980s, as well as the vast proliferation of staff personnel and support services provided to Connecticut lawmakers. Moreover, many state lawmakers, although still considered "citizen legislators," have in reality become full-time professional legislators. A sizeable number of state lawmakers always seem to be present at the state Capitol, regardless of whether the General Assembly is in session.

A State-of-the Art Legislative Office Building

A League of Women Voters' tour of the Connecticut state Capitol is the most instructive way of learning about the physical and operational dimensions of the state Capitol.[2] The tour will begin in the building adjacent to the Capitol, what is known as the Legislative Office Building or LOB. A 500-foot underground concourse connects the LOB. with the main Capitol building. Completed in 1987, the five-story LOB. is one of the most technologically sophisticated legislative office buildings in the United States. The offices of state lawmakers and legislative support staff are housed in the LOB. The ornate building is also home to ten state-of-the-art committee hearing rooms. Hearing rooms, the offices of state lawmakers, and the two legislative chambers in the Capitol building are all interconnected through an intricate and complex system of electronic cables and computer monitors. Lawmakers unable to attend legislative hearings or floor debate can follow proceedings on monitors designed for this purpose. The technology of the LOB was also designed to serve the needs of the Connecticut public. Should public attendance at hearings exceed seating capacity, video screens and monitors located in additional hearing rooms permit the public to observe the proceedings. The LOB. is lavish in its décor and architectural detail, perhaps to the point of extravagance. A question sometimes asked by tour participants, not surprisingly, is "how much did this building cost?" The answer is $67 million.

The LOB, more than any other government building at the state Capitol, symbolizes Connecticut's long-term commitment to meeting the varied and proliferating demands of the state's 3.4 million inhabitants. The technology offered to state lawmakers most certainly enhances the legislature's capacity for efficient and responsive lawmaking. While technological support alone may not guarantee effective legislative performance, such technology is nevertheless a tremendous asset for the purposes of knowing, and responding to, the needs of the Connecticut public.

Support Offices and Legislative Staff

In addition to sophisticated technology and a state-of-the-art legislative office complex, state lawmakers have also come to depend quite heavily on state employed personnel located in legislative support offices and legislative staffs. The activity of support office and staff personnel has in recent years become indispensable with respect to assisting state legislators with the many complex dimensions associated with lawmaking.

Twelve nonpartisan support offices, which report to the Joint Committee on Legislative Management, provide an array of critical services to state lawmakers. Four offices in particular serve major legislative functions. The Office of Legislative Research serves as the research and information arm of the state legislature. The Office of Fiscal Analysis analyzes the fiscal dimensions and financial implications of legislative proposals. The Program Review and Investigations Committee assists lawmakers with the difficult task of administrative oversight. This involves the periodic review of executive agency activity to determine if in fact agencies are implementing laws in accordance with the intent of the law. The Legislative Commissioners Office offers consultation to lawmakers on the legal language of bills and potential conflicts between legislative statutes and the Connecticut Constitution. Non-partisan offices are in close and daily contact with state lawmakers throughout the legislative session and have become integral to the development and implementation of laws. In 2006, non-partisan personnel accounted for 54 percent of all full-time staff at the state Capitol.[3]

Legislative staffs, which are also under the direction of the Joint Committee on Legislative Management, have also proliferated at the state Capitol, a trend similar to that of the United States Congress. Like congressional staffs, legislative staffs in Connecticut have assumed multiple functions related to lawmaking. Legislative staffs at the Capitol have been established to assist legislative standing committees and, more generally, the political parties within the legislature. Even the most casual observer cannot help but notice the highly visible and fast-paced movement of legislative staff personnel throughout the corridors and offices of the LOB and Capitol building. Legislative staff workers, unlike those who work in support offices, are classified as partisan staff. Partisan staff workers currently account for 46 percent of all full-time personnel at the state Capitol.[4]

The partisan legislative staffs are formally connected to the four party caucuses in the state Capitol: the House Democrats, the House Republicans, the Senate Democrats, and the Senate Republicans. Some staffers work directly for a caucus, while others are assigned to the twenty-two legislative committees. Some staffers work at the Capitol in a full-time, year-round capacity, while others are full-time employees only while the legislature is in session. Seventy-six individuals are full-time committee staffers while the legislature is in session and approximately twenty-five to thirty individuals are full-time throughout the year. The extent to which legislative staffers have become central to the operation of the state legislature is best expressed in the words of legislative aides Gary Turco and Jason Bowsza. Turco, a legislative aide to Speaker of the House James Amann, described a staff worker's job in these terms: "Elected officials need to be knowledgeable in a variety of areas that affect the lives of constituents. Staff members become experts in different policy areas and serve as a constant source of information for elected officials." Jason Bowsza, a legislative aide to state senator Bill Finch, co-chair of the General Assembly's Environment Committee, offers this perspective on the role of a staff worker:

Staffers in the Connecticut state senate generally focus on constituent work, as well as issuing press releases, tracking legislation, attending meetings with lobbyists and offering advice on policy and politics to our senators. Each staffer serves their senator in a unique way, but always following their senator's example.[5]

Generally speaking, the number of support personnel at the Connecticut State Capitol has become quite significant. As of 2006, there are more than 570 paid support personnel working at the Connecticut state Capitol during the legislative session. This figure includes 412 year round, full-time non-partisan and partisan employees, and 160 full-time "temporary/sessional/interim" staff. Add to this figure the 120 or so non-paid legislative interns who also work at the state Capitol during the legislative session and one discovers that Connecticut's 187 lawmakers are assisted in one form or another by close to 700 support personnel.[6] The number of persons now working at the Connecticut state Capitol suggests a state legislature inundated with diverse, complicated, and pressing demands. The number of support personnel further suggests a state legislature prepared and willing to confront the complex policy challenges of the twenty-first century.

The Capitol

The underground escalator, known as the "Concourse," connects the Legislative Office Building to the state Capitol building. It is within the historic state Capitol building where one finds the two legislative chambers: the House of Representatives and the Senate. The House and Senate collectively comprise the Connecticut General Assembly. The offices of state legislative leaders, the offices of Governor and Lieutenant Governor, as well as the offices of the constitutional officers, such as the Secretary of State are also located in the Capitol building. It is in the state Capitol where the laws that govern the state of Connecticut are formally introduced and passed. The state Capitol building, completed in 1879, is registered as a National Historic Landmark. Prior to construction of the Capitol building, the Old State House in downtown Hartford served as the Capitol building.[7]

Like the United States Congress and state legislatures across the land, with the exception of Nebraska, which is unicameral, the Connecticut state legislature is a bicameral institution. The House of Representatives, located on the second floor of the Capitol building, is at times referred to as the "lower house," and the Senate, located on the third floor, is sometimes referred to as the "upper house." Such terms however have become someone antiquated within the lexicon of legislative politics. Although both chambers are equal in power and both assume responsibility for passing laws, they are nevertheless very different from one another in terms of structural design, legislative procedure, and formality.

The House of Representatives: The People's Chamber

Located on the second floor of the state Capitol building, the Connecticut House of Representatives is in theory where the passions and will of the Connecticut citizenry are most closely represented. Following the 2000 federal census, state legislative districts were redrawn and adjusted to rectify population imbalance and account for population growth. Population growth was rather minimal compared to states in other regions of the country, most notably the South and West. For the first decade of the twenty-first century, House legislative districts were redrawn to contain approximately 29,000 people. As previously discussed in Chapter Two, the Supreme Court cases of *Baker v. Carr* (1962), *Reynolds v. Sims* (1964), and *Butterworth v. Dempsey* (1964) have ensured that state legislative districts consist of roughly the same number of people.

Every ten years, following the federal census, a reapportionment committee established within the state legislature is assigned the responsibility of redrawing legislative districts to reflect the "one-person one-vote" principle. Although one discovers elements of "gerrymandering" in the legislative reapportionment process, a term used to describe the redrawing of district lines to benefit the reelection chances of the party in power, Connecticut's reapportionment process is for the most part fair. Amendment XVI of the Connecticut Constitution, which describes in detail the entire reapportionment procedure, requires that the final draft of a reapportionment plan be approved by at least two-thirds of each house of the state legislature. Thus, the two-thirds vote inherently prevents the majority party, currently the Democrats, from rendering the minority party, currently the Republicans, powerless during the reapportionment process. The two-thirds rule allows the minority party in the state legislature to veto a reapportionment plan perceived as grossly unfair. In the 2006 election, the Democrats captured two-thirds of the seats in both the House and Senate. Whether they will still control two-thirds of the seats during the next reapportionment process following the 2010 federal census remains to be seen. Should the legislature fail to adopt a reapportionment plan, a bipartisan commission will be convened to resolve the matter and arrive at a compromise. In the event the commission fails to develop a compromise plan, the state supreme court under the direction of the chief justice will supervise and coordinate the reapportionment process.

According to the state constitution, a state representative must be at least eighteen years of age. Representatives are elected to a term of two years, with no limit placed on reelection. Since 1967, the Connecticut House of Representatives, and subsequently the state's legislative agenda, has been under the control of the Democratic Party. Name recognition of House incumbents, effective use of legislative staffs for constituent service, fundraising capabilities of incumbents, the fact that Connecticut is a "Blue" state, as well as reapportionment and elements of gerrymandering have secured for the Democratic Party many years of political control over the state House of Representatives. The only exceptions to this long period of Democratic dominance were the legislative sessions of 1973-74 and 1985-86. President Nixon's landslide reelection in 1972 and President Reagan's reelection landslide in 1984 resulted in political coattails for Republican state legislative candidates and short-lived Republican majorities in the House. Following the legislative election of 2006, the Democratic Party in Connecticut controlled 107 seats (71 percent), while the Republican Party occupied 44 seats (29 percent).

House Leadership

A small group of party leaders controls the legislative business of the House of Representatives. The key leadership posts include the Speaker of the House, the House majority leader, House majority whip, House minority leader, and House minority whip.

The Speaker of the House is the presiding officer of the entire House of Representatives. The Speaker controls floor proceedings, interprets parliamentary rules of procedure, recognizes lawmakers during floor debate, and refers bills to committee.[8] Unlike other legislative leaders in the House, the Speaker is required to perform a dual role. The Speaker is first and foremost the chief representative and symbol of the Connecticut House of Representatives. In this capacity, the Speaker must ensure fairness during floor debate and, more important, protect the autonomy and integrity of the House chamber. As the presiding officer of the House of Representatives, the Speaker is formally elected by a vote of the entire House membership, although he or she is always a member of the majority party. The Speaker, therefore, will undoubtedly advance the interests and agenda of the majority party, while at the same time ensuring fairness to the opposition party. The post of Speaker of the House is a complex office. Speakers are normally individuals with many years of legislative experience, political savvy, and a broad network of allies within the House chamber. For example, the current Speaker of the House, James Amann, an eight-term Democrat from Milford, served as Assistant Majority Leader, Deputy Majority Whip, and House Majority Leader prior to his election as House Speaker. Speaker Amann describes the complexity of the Speaker's role in this way: "Assuring proper rules and procedure are followed, especially when it comes to constitutional questions, is the top priority. The Speaker is much like a referee, guaranteeing fairness and non-partisan debate from the dais."[9]

For many years, tradition dictated that the Speaker of the House would serve for one two-year term. The one-term tradition ended in 1971 with the reelection of Democratic House Speaker William Ratchford to a second consecutive term.[10] Since Ratchford's reelection, it is not unusual for Speakers to serve two consecutive terms, with two terms now considered the norm for House Speakers.

The extent to which state lawmakers guard against encroachment of the two-term tradition was more than evident in 1989, when Speaker of the House Irving J. Stolberg, a Democrat from New Haven, decided to seek a third consecutive term. In response to this unprecedented development, an anti-Stolberg faction of Democrats, who had become extremely weary of Stolberg's leadership style, liberal politics, and political ambitions, secretly colluded with House Republicans to deny the controversial Speaker the necessary majority needed for reelection. This most unusual political alliance of anti-Stolberg Democrats and Republicans, unthinkable in years past, coalesced to elect Democrat Richard Balducci to the post of Speaker. This was the first time in Connecticut history that a Speaker of the House was elected by a bipartisan coalition of Democrats and Republicans. The bipartisan alliance was further proof that party membership no longer dictates legislative behavior in the Connecticut General Assembly. Republicans working with Democrats to elect the Speaker is in some respects a reflection of a much larger phenomenon regarding the declining significance of political parties as governing instruments.

The House majority leader is the floor manager for the majority party and serves as the key spokesperson for the majority party's legislative agenda. The majority whip is responsible for maximizing attendance during legislative roll calls and for persuading party members to work as a team. The term "whip" is an old British term used to describe the person responsible for managing the foxhounds during a fox hunt: the "whipper-in" of the hounds. The term was subsequently applied to those persons responsible for promoting party cohesion within the British Parliament.[11] Both the majority leader and majority whip are elected in the party caucus prior to the start of a new legislature.

The minority leader and minority whip have functions similar to those of the majority leader and majority whip. Representing the legislative agenda of the minority party, speaking on behalf of the minority party, and maximizing party cohesion among minority party members are among the principal tasks associated with the minority party leadership posts. Minority party leaders are elected in the minority party caucus at the start of a new legislature.

In addition to the chief leadership posts within the majority and minority parties, both party caucuses in the House of Representatives elect deputy leaders and several assistant leaders. Deputy and assistant leaders perform a number of specific legislative tasks designed to help promote the agenda of the party hierarchy. Deputy and assistant leadership positions are normally reserved for lawmakers who have demonstrated loyalty to the party's legislative leadership. In the view of one lawmaker I spoke with, who wished to remain anonymous, the post of assistant leader is also useful for the purpose of advancing political careers: the title is impressive, yet the position seldom involves substantive responsibilities.

Any House Democrat or House Republican who wishes to introduce a legislative proposal is advised to secure the backing of legislative leaders within his or her respective party. In the Connecticut House of Representatives, a significant portion of the legislative agenda is controlled by a relatively small hierarchy of legislative leaders. Freshmen lawmakers are quick to learn that legislative proposals, including those of great merit, must obtain the approval of their party's legislative leadership in order for the proposal to be deemed viable. Moreover, the legislative agenda is established fairly early in the legislative session, and for all intents and purposes reflects the goals of legislative leaders. This is not to suggest that newly-elected representative are powerless with respect to lawmaking. Freshmen lawmakers do introduce bills and receive important committee assignments. However, to have a meaningful voice in the Connecticut House of Representatives, it is essential for the newly-elected lawmaker to work with and gain the support of the party's legislative leadership. The party's leadership has the authority to filter legislative proposals.

The State Senate: A Governing Council

The state Senate is located on the third floor of the state Capitol building. With respect to structure, procedure, and custom, the state Senate is quite unlike the House of Representatives. Compared to the House, the Senate is a much smaller chamber consisting of only thirty-six members, less than one-fourth the size. In terms of structure, the Senate has the appearance of a deliberative council, with senators positioned in a large circle, as opposed to the formal rows of desks found in the House chamber. In the House of Representatives, the two parties sit on opposite sides of the aisle, which gives the House chamber a more partisan flair with respect to appearance. In the Senate chamber, senators are positioned according to the number of their senatorial district, which allows Democratic and Republican senators to sit, discuss bills, and vote on proposals while they are adjacent to one another. The state Senate is thus a very different chamber compared to the House with regard to collegiality.

Like House members, state senators are elected to two-year terms, with no limit placed on reelection. Any individual who seeks a Senate seat must be a minimum of 18 years of age. A Connecticut state senator currently represents a legislative district consisting of approximately 91,000 persons. In both population and geographical size, senatorial districts are substantially larger than House districts. State senators must therefore understand the needs of diverse constituencies in several contiguous towns. Compared to House members, senators, due to the nature of their districts, must acquire a broader working knowledge of state and local policy matters.

As in the state House of Representatives, the Democratic Party has controlled the business of the state Senate for many years. Democratic dominance appears to have begun as far back as 1959, with only three exceptions, 1973-74 and 1985-86, the same years in which the Republican Party won a majority of seats in the state House, and 1995-96, a reflection of the 1994 congressional election in which the Republicans gained control over the U.S. House of Representatives. Following the 2006 legislative election, the

Democrats controlled 24 seats (67 percent), while the Republicans held 12 seats (33 percent).

Similar to the House of Representatives, incumbents in the state Senate tend to be reelected with relative ease. Like House incumbents, incumbents in the Senate can employ legislative staffs for constituency service and have higher name recognition compared to challengers. Moreover, Senate incumbents have a clear advantage over challengers with regard to fundraising. Thus, many state senators have safe seats. The power of incumbency and the emergence of safe legislative districts in both House and Senate elections does not bode well for two-party competition. The decline of competitive legislative districts in Connecticut was treated in detail in Chapter Three. Landslide elections and safe seats have become the norm in state legislative elections.

Legislative process in the state Senate is more informal than that of the House of Representatives, and there is more reliance on legislative customs rather than strict parliamentary procedure. Unlike the party caucuses in the House, the party caucuses in the Senate are where many crucial policy decisions are made. Wayne Swanson's definitive study of the Connecticut state legislature discovered that it was in the party caucus, not on the floor of the Senate, where major decisions were reached regarding the fate of bills. Due to the intimacy of the Senate chamber, freshmen senators, compared to their counterparts in the House, were also discovered by Swanson to have more of a voice in the legislative process.[12] Judge Robert Satter, a former state representative, confirms Swanson's observation of the Senate caucus and notes that compared to the House, more bills are placed on the Consent Calendar: "The Senate usually finishes its work first and waits around for the House to send up business."[13]

Senate Leadership

Although the state Senate is a more intimate and informal legislative chamber than the House, and freshmen senators exert more impact in the lawmaking process than House freshmen, there is nevertheless a small group of party leaders in the Senate who exercise considerable power over the chamber's internal affairs. Senate leaders, like House leaders, perform important managerial and leadership functions.

The president of the state Senate is the state's lieutenant governor. As the official presiding officer of the Senate, the lieutenant governor interprets rules of Senate procedure, recognizes senators who wish to speak, and refers bills to legislative committees. The lieutenant governor only votes in the event of a tie. Unlike the Speaker of the House, the lieutenant governor's position in the Senate is more ceremonial than political. The lieutenant governor is elected with the governor on the same ticket, and thus presides over the Senate by virtue of his or her constitutional position. The lieutenant governor is not elected from among the ranks of the Senate membership, nor while presiding over the Senate is he or she considered a member of the "club." The lieutenant governor will serve as the "eyes and ears" of the governor with respect to the business of the Senate, but the lieutenant governor normally does not direct the business of the Senate.

The true power in the Connecticut Senate is found in the several leadership posts elected by the two party caucuses. These posts include the president of the Senate pro tempore (usually referred to as the pro tem), the majority leader, majority whip, minority leader, and minority whip. The senate pro tem presides over the Senate when the lieutenant governor is absent. The pro tem is elected by the majority party caucus at the start of a new legislative session, and normally steers the agenda of the majority party. Although the pro tem at times is expected to speak for the entire Senate, the reality of the matter is that he or she is the leader of the majority party. The pro tem has considerable control over Senate committee appointments, exercises control over the legislative agenda, and without a doubt is the pivotal and most powerful figure in the entire Senate chamber.

The majority leader, majority whip, minority leader, and minority whip perform functions similar to their counterparts in the House chamber. Elected by their respected party caucuses, the leaders and whips represent, guide, and help manage their party's legislative agenda.

The majority leader and majority whip work closely with the pro tem in advancing the agenda of the majority party. Like the House chamber, there are also several deputy and assistant leaders in the state Senate.

Tools of Legislative Leadership

The days of party bosses operating "behind-the-scenes" and controlling legislative voting behavior with patronage jobs and party organization money are no longer present in Connecticut politics. The new era is marked by candidate-centered politics, which manifests itself in elected lawmakers who do not feel beholden to party leaders. George Gallo was the chairman of the Republican Party in Connecticut, yet Gallo did not control the voting behavior of Republican state lawmakers. Nancy DiNardo is the chairwoman of the Democratic Party in Connecticut, yet DiNardo does not control the voting behavior of Democratic state lawmakers. State legislative leaders elected in party caucuses are also limited in terms of persuading and influencing the voting behavior of rank-and-file lawmakers. There is only so much the Speaker of the House, Senate pro tem and the majority and minority leaders can do to foster party teamwork in the Connecticut General Assembly.

Nevertheless, despite the decline of party authority in the lawmaking process, there are mechanisms or "tools" that a party's legislative leaders can employ to cultivate a network of political support among party members. Such tools, when skillfully and strategically employed, can have the effect of drawing rank-and-file lawmakers closer to the goals of the party hierarchy. Two important sources of persuasion appear to be preferential appointments to legislative standing committees and the distribution of campaign dollars to legislative candidates.

Committee Appointments

Appointments to legislative standing committees remain one of the most important sources of leverage exercised by party leaders in both chambers of the General Assembly. By serving on key standing committees, House and Senate members can often serve the needs of their constituents in a most direct fashion. Indeed, the policy areas that fall under the jurisdiction of standing committees often have direct bearing on a representative's or senator's constituents. A House or Senate member with many teachers in his or her legislative district would necessarily want to serve on the legislature's Education Committee. A lawmaker who represents a legislative district with many small businesses would most likely prefer an appointment to the legislature's Commerce Committee. At the same time, there are standing committees that go well beyond the unique needs of individual districts and affect the state's population as a whole. The Appropriations Committee and the Finance, Revenue, and Bonding Committee are examples of legislative committees that have statewide impact. Lawmakers who support the goals of legislative leaders are thus rewarded with choice committee assignments.

Campaign Finance Committees

Another leadership tool for House and Senate leaders emanates from the campaign finance committees that have been established by both parties in the House and Senate chambers. Campaign finance committees were established in the Connecticut state legislature to help finance the costs associated with House and Senate campaigns. To help alleviate the increasing demands of fund raising, campaign finance committees were established for the express purpose of supplementing the campaign budgets of House and Senate candidates. Legislative campaign finance committees are under the control of legislative leaders and the leaders determine which legislative candidates will be the recipients of campaign dollars. This is not to suggest that legislative candidates depend exclusively on legislative campaign committees to win election or reelection. This is now an era of candidate-centered politics, and legislative candidates depend on their own network of individual contributors and special interest groups to finance campaigns. Nevertheless, party leaders in the legislature do distribute substantial sums of money to legislative candidates, normally to those candidates in highly competitive contests. By distributing campaign dollars to candidates in closely contested elections, legislative leaders are able to cultivate a network of loyalists who feel obliged to support the agenda of the legislative hierarchy. There is a sense of appreciation and indebtedness that follows from campaign assistance.

Legislative campaign finance committees in the Connecticut General Assembly exist in two different forms. One form is directly associated with and established by individual legislative leaders. These are the legislative leadership PACs (LLPs) that appear to have proliferated within the state Capitol. The leadership PACs normally have partisan titles, yet the reality of the matter is that they have been established to serve the goals of individual legislative leaders. Legislative Leadership PACs are a growing presence in the Connecticut legislature, as well as legislative assemblies in other states.[14]

The second form of campaign finance assistance emerges from the broader and more party-oriented legislative campaign finance committees. Such committees have been formed by both parties in both legislative chambers. The legislative campaign finance committees are different from the Legislative Leadership PACs in that campaign dollars are normally distributed among a broader array of legislative candidates, as opposed to a select group of candidates. Some legislative candidates are the recipients of more assistance than others, but in general there seems to be more concern with improving the strength and competitiveness of the party as a whole compared to the more selective contributions from the Leadership PACs. Taken together, campaign dollars from the legislative leadership PACs and dollars distributed from the legislative campaign finance committees are instrumental in cultivating allegiance to the party's legislative hierarchy. When added to the power over committee appointments, it becomes clear that legislative leaders, while by no means omnipotent, still have political tools at their disposal to lead and direct the internal affairs of the Connecticut state legislature.

The Lawmaking Process

Lawmaking in the Connecticut General Assembly, as in all legislatures, is an intriguing affair. Practically all bills introduced into the state legislature encounter hurdles, unexpected obstacles, and in most cases "brick walls." Indeed, it is more common for bills to die in the Connecticut General Assembly than to be passed. To surmount political opposition, proponents of bills must skillfully forge legislative coalitions, negotiate compromises on key sections of bills, and be willing to cut deals to placate and appease the political opposition. No textbook description can ever completely capture what happens behind the scenes during the passage of a bill, and at times it is perhaps better not to know. Indeed, one is reminded of the old adage often attributed to the German Chancellor Otto von Bismarck: "If you like laws and sausages, you should never watch either one being made."[15]

As described in Chapter One, the Tenth Amendment to the United States Constitution reserves to states those powers that are not delegated to the federal government, as well as those that are not specifically prohibited to the states. The policy areas in which the Connecticut state legislature can legislate are not specifically enumerated in the state constitution, thus allowing the state legislature considerable latitude to legislate on a wide variety of issues, albeit within constitutional limits. The policies of education, housing, transportation, criminal justice, and environmental protection are examples of policy areas that belong to the Connecticut state legislature. Policy areas such as taxation and appropriations also belong to the state legislature, although such powers are exercised concurrently with the federal government. The Connecticut state legislature, in other words, can pass many laws in many policy areas, as long as such policies do not belong exclusively to the federal government. The state legislature, for example, cannot pass laws that regulate interstate commerce or trade with foreign nations, nor can the legislature pass laws involving foreign policy. Such areas, as defined in the federal constitution, are the domain of the federal government, not the states.

Table Two documents the number of proposed House and Senate bills in the Connecticut state legislature from 2000 through 2005, as well as the raw number and percentage of bills eventually signed into law by the governor. The reader should be aware that the Connecticut state legislature during odd-numbered years is in session from the Wednesday following the first Monday in January to the Wednesday following the first Monday in June, slightly more than five months. In even-numbered years, the state legislature is in session from the Wednesday following the first Monday in February to the Wednesday following the first Monday in May, slightly more than three months. Sessions conducted during even-numbered years are commonly referred to as "short sessions." Legislative sessions during odd-numbered years are thus longer and hence the volume of proposed bills tends to be greater compared to the sessions in even-numbered years. It should also be noted that only bills related to fiscal matters may be introduced in the even-numbered years.

Table 2
Proposed Bills and Public Acts
2000-05 Regular Session

Year	Proposed Bills	Public Acts	% Passed
2000	1812	402	22%
2001	3765	470	12%
2002	1812	382	21%
2003	3648	274	8%
2004	1618	518	32%
2005	3655	481	13%

Source: Law Department, Connecticut State Library.

As the data show, whether it is a large volume of proposed bills in the odd-numbered years or the smaller number of bills in even numbered years, a relatively small percentage of proposals are ever enacted into law. From 2000-05, an average of 18 percent of proposed bills eventually made it into law.

The number of proposed bills tends to be greater in the House chamber because the House contains 151 members, compared to 36 members in the Senate. Hence there is more legislative business transacted in the House. However, although the number of proposed bills is higher in the House, and while the House chamber tends to pass a greater quantity of bills, the percentage of bills that are passed in the House is quite similar to that of the state Senate. Table Three documents the number of proposed bills in both chambers, as well as the number and percentage of bills passed by each chamber.

Table 3
Proposed and Passed Bills in the House and Senate Chambers
2000-05 Regular Session

	House			Senate		
	Proposed	Passed	%	Proposed	Passed	%
2000	930	146	16%	640	98	15%
2001	2051	146	7%	1459	163	11%
2002	811	108	13%	677	126	19%
2003	1969	161	8%	1333	113	8%
2004	690	162	23%	633	189	30%
2005	2004	167	8%	1386	137	10%

Source: Law Department, Connecticut State Library.

The Committees

Although bills can die in several places, it is clear that the legislative standing committees in the Connecticut General Assembly are the "graveyard" for the vast majority of legislative proposals. Most proposed bills die in legislative standing committee and never make it to the House or Senate floors. As Swanson notes:

It is often surprising to the new lawmaker to see the number of bills referred to committees that are never discussed and simply die in committee. The time factor in the legislature is such that committees, in conjunction with leadership, must select the bills which they consider the most important, denying to the "less important" legislation a place on the committee's agenda. It often takes a number of assembly sessions for a bill which the leadership considers to be of "marginal importance" to get a committee hearing. The new legislator should not be discouraged if his bills do not make it out of committee the first time that they are introduced.[16]

Legislative standing committees in the Connecticut General Assembly are joint committees. Membership on standing committees consists of members from both the House and Senate chambers. Each standing committee is headed by co-chairpersons. One co-chairperson is appointed from the House by the House Speaker, while one is appointed from the Senate by the Senate president pro tempore. The co-chairpersons alternate as presiding officers over committee hearings. Each co-chairperson is a member of the majority party in his or her respective legislative chamber. Appointments to joint committees are based on a proportional formula, with seats allocated to members based on the strength of both parties in the House and Senate.

At present, there are twenty-five joint committees in the Connecticut General Assembly. This number includes the permanent standing committees responsible for passing bills, the small number of permanent committees that do not process bills but instead are assigned specific non-legislative tasks, as well as the non-permanent select committees established to perform very special functions related to narrow policy areas.

True power in the General Assembly lies within the legislative standing committees. Lawmakers normally serve on two or perhaps three legislative standing committees during a legislative session. Examples of legislative standing committees include the Appropriations Committee, the Commerce Committee, and the Transportation Committee. The political careers of state lawmakers are advanced by serving on key standing committees, and it is within the standing committees that the laws affecting the state of Connecticut are ultimately shaped.

Legislative Procedure

Proposed bills have many origins.[17] Bills can originate with the governor, individual lawmakers, lobbyists, executive branch officials, or individual constituents. For a bill to be introduced into either the House or Senate chamber, there must be a lawmaker or group of lawmakers who sponsor the bill. A bill can be introduced into either chamber of the state legislature.

Once a bill is introduced, it is then forwarded to one of the legislative standing committees cited above. Assuming that the bill has a modicum of support, the committee will schedule a public hearing on the bill in one of the committee rooms within the Legislative Office Building. The general public is allowed to attend such hearings and individuals along with group representatives are allowed to voice their concerns before committee members. Following the committee hearing and often much discussion and debate among committee members, the committee will vote on the bill. Should the committee vote against the bill, it will issue an "Unfavorable Report." Should the committee vote in favor of the bill, it will issue a "Favorable Report," or "JF" ("Joint Favorable") Report. Should the committee decide to take no action on the bill, the bill will be "boxed" and automatically die. When the committee decides to box a bill, it will issue "No Report." A simple majority vote among committee members is needed for the bill to pass a standing committee.

Once a bill has passed the committee stage of the lawmaking process, it is then placed on the legislative calendar. Bills deemed non-controversial by members of the standing committee and that are expected to pass the House and Senate floors without discussion are placed on the Consent Calendar. All other bills are assigned to the regular legislative calendar and scheduled for floor action.

Bills that pass the standing committee stage of the process and that require funding, as most do, are forwarded to the

Appropriations Committee or the Committee on Finance, Revenue, and Bonding. The "money committees," as they are known, decide whether or not to authorize funds for the program outlined in the bill. Practically all legislative programs require funding, and it is the responsibility of the money committees to explore and discuss the financial ramifications of the proposed policy. The money committees have the authority to pass or reject the bill. Should funding be denied, the bill will die at this stage of the process. Should the money committees approve funding for the proposed program, the bill will then be forwarded to the Office of Fiscal Analysis for a detailed financial analysis. Once the work of the Office of Fiscal Analysis is completed, the bill will proceed to the House and Senate floors for a vote. Prior to the floor vote in both chambers, amendments might be added to the bill and lawmakers can engage in extensive floor debate. Should the bill pass the House and Senate floors in two different versions, a conference committee will be convened to resolve House and Senate differences. A conference committee is a special joint committee assembled from both chambers to iron out the differences between the two legislative chambers. Should the bill pass the conference committee and be approved by both legislative chambers, it is then forwarded to the governor for executive action.

The Governor's Desk

The concept of checks and balances is most evident when a bill passed by the legislature is sent to the governor. During a normal legislative session, the governor has a total of five calendar days to respond to a passed bill. During this period, the governor can sign the bill into law, in which case the bill will become an official Public Act, or the governor can veto the proposed legislation. Should the governor veto the bill, it will be returned to the legislature with the governor's veto message. A gubernatorial veto can be overridden by a two-thirds vote of each legislative chamber, although this is extremely difficult to do. If the governor does not take any action within five days of receiving the bill, and the legislature is still in session, the bill will automatically become law without his or her signature. Should the governor not take action after the legislature had adjourned, then the bill will automatically become law without his or her signature after fifteen days.

In addition to exercising a regular veto, Connecticut's governor is afforded the constitutional power to exercise the line-item veto. The line-item veto can be employed only in conjunction with appropriations legislation. The governor can veto specific spending items in an appropriations bill, while signing the remainder of the bill into law. Forty-five state governors can exercise the line-item veto. Like the regular veto, the line-item veto can be overridden by a two-thirds vote of both legislative chambers. In theory, the line-item veto is supposed to allow state governors the opportunity to more carefully scrutinize and control wasteful state spending. Although a constitutional power of the Connecticut governor, Connecticut governors rarely exercise the line-item veto. However, much to the surprise of many lawmakers, on June 4, 2007, Governor Rell exercised the line-item veto in conjunction with a proposed energy bill. The governor signed the energy bill into law, but vetoed two of the bill's sections concerning appropriations

The veto is one of the most powerful tools exercised by the Connecticut governor, and is perhaps one of the most direct methods of constraining the actions of the state legislature. Table Four documents the extent to which the gubernatorial veto has been employed in Connecticut from 2000-05.

Table 4
Gubernatorial Vetoes: 2000-05

Year	Vetoes	Overridden
2000	3	0
2001	3	0
2002	3	0
2003	2	0
2004	12	0
2005	9	0

Source: Law Department, Connecticut State Library.

As the evidence suggests, despite the fact that the governorship has been under the control of a Republican governor for many years and the legislature dominated by Democrats, the veto has been used somewhat sparingly. Years 2004 and 2005 appear to be the exception, rather than the norm. Both recent Republican governors, Rowland and Rell, have governed the state of Connecticut from the center of the political spectrum. Compromising, bargaining, and cooperating with a Democratic-controlled legislature, rather than antagonizing the opposition has been the norm at the state Capitol.

The governor of Connecticut plays a pivotal and equal role in the lawmaking process, and the veto power is one of the most important methods of shaping and controlling the outcome of public policy. At the same time, however, the veto is not by any means the only power exercised by the governor. Indeed, the scope of gubernatorial power has clearly grown in recent decades to the point where the governorship in Connecticut now resembles the American presidency, only on a smaller scale. The centrality of the state governorship within the context of state politics and the multi-faceted nature of the modern governorship are addressed in the following chapter.

Notes

1.   Expectations for state governments are quite high throughout the U.S. Fifty-two percent of persons polled expressed the view that their governor and state legislature care more about the problems that affect their lives personally, while 36 percent believed the federal level of government was the most caring. The same poll discovered that more Americans view the local and state levels of government as more likely to "get more done" compared to the federal level of government. "Immigration, Federalism," Andres McKenna Research, January 15-25, 2004. N=800 registered voters. Poll data cited in Thomas R. Dye and Susan A. MacManus, *Politics in States and Communities,* 12th edition (Upper Saddle River, NJ: Pearson Education, 2007), p. 86.

2.   The League of Women Voters have a booth in the Legislative Office Building and provide excellent tours of the LOB and the state

Capitol. The tours are tailored to the age and particular interests of the audience. Reservations for tours are required.

3. Information on support offices and staff supplied through phone conversation with Jim Tracy, personnel administrator for Joint Committee on Legislative Management, October 6, 2006.

4. Jim Tracy, October 6, 2006.

5. Quotations from legislative aides Gary Turco and Jason Bowsza obtained from e-mails on, respectively, August 30 and September 1, 2006.

6. Jim Tracy, October 6, 2006.

7. Jane Zarem, ed., *The Connecticut Citizen's Handbook* 3rd. ed. (Chester, CT: Globe Pequot Press, 1987), p. 35.

8. Wayne Swanson, *Lawmaking in Connecticut: The General Assembly* (New London, CT: Connecticut College, 1978), p. 42.

9. Quote obtained via e-mail from Speaker of the House James Amann, September 5, 2006.

10. Swanson, *Lawmaking in Connecticut*, p. 42.

11. Randall B. Ripley, *Congress: Process and Policy*, 4th ed. (New York: W.W. Norton, 1988), p. 64

12. Swanson, *Lawmaking in Connecticut*, p. 40.

13. Robert Satter, *Under the Gold Dome: An Insider's Look at the Connecticut State Legislature* (New Haven: Connecticut Conference of Municipalities, 2004), p. 108.

14. See Daniel M. Shea, *Transforming Democracy: Legislative Campaign Committees and Political Parties* (Albany: State University of New York Press, 1995).

15. This quotation is often attributed to Otto von Bismarck, the "Iron Chancellor" of Germany from 1871-1890, although the original source of the statement is unverified, according to *Bartleby Quotations;* online at www.bartleby.com/73/996.htm.

16. Swanson, *Lawmaking in Connecticut*, p. 64.

17. A brief but excellent summary of legislative procedure can be found in "This Is Your General Assembly," published by the Connecticut General Assembly, 1999-2000. The website for Connecticut government contains an outstanding "Citizen Guide" covering numerous facets of the legislative process, including legislative procedure; see www.cga.ct.gov/asp/menu/citizen.asp.

CHAPTER SIX

The Governor's Office and Judiciary

The State Governorship

The governor presides over the executive branch. Elected for a four-year term, with no limitation on reelection, the Connecticut governor, now more than ever, is expected to be the driving force behind the policy-making process. In recent decades, the citizens of Connecticut have come to expect a governor who is creative, energetic, and an imaginative problem solver. Like public expectations of the American president, the American people have high expectations of those who occupy state governorships. The following summary succinctly captures this orientation:

> Governors are expected to be the leading cheerleaders for their states. They are expected to attract business and jobs, to set the political tone, to manage state affairs. They serve as the primary face and voice of government during natural disasters or other crises. With this much power, of course, comes a great deal of expectation. If a state is not doing well – if it is losing more jobs than its neighbors during a recession, for example, or is running a budget deficit – voters and the media will hold the governor responsible. They are like mini-presidents in each state.[1]

The Connecticut governor's formal powers unfold from the state constitution. Moreover, the constitutional duties of the

Connecticut governor described in Article IV are quite substantial, and in many ways parallel those of the American president. The parallel is common in most states. As Louis W. Koenig states, "If a typical early governor were compared with a typical contemporary governor, the influence of the presidency upon gubernatorial change would become evident."[2] Similar to that of the president, the governor in Connecticut is expected to "wear many hats" and have the ability to perform several tasks simultaneously. The 1965 Constitution was crafted in such a way as to create an empowered governorship.

To begin with, the state constitution assigns an important legislative duty to the governor. In this capacity, the governor is allowed to introduce bills to the state legislature, sign bills into law, and exercise the power of veto. The constitution also requires the governor to deliver a "State of the Government" address to the state legislature. This address, more popularly known as the "State of the State" address, attracts extensive media coverage. Like the president's "State of the Union" message, the "State of the State" address broadly outlines the governor's legislative agenda for the forthcoming legislative session. The governor's address is what sets the legislative process in motion.

In addition to broad legislative responsibilities, the constitution requires the governor to perform a range of executive duties. As the state's chief executive officer, the governor is expected to "faithfully" execute the laws of the state. In this regard, it is the governor's legal responsibility to oversee the implementation of state laws and state judicial rulings. Gubernatorial appointments within the executive branch are crucial in this respect, as the successful execution of laws depend heavily on the ability, motivation, and orientation of personnel working within executive agencies and commissions. Under the Rell administration, approximately thirty individuals are directly appointed by the governor to serve on the governor's personal staff. Such staff positions include, among others, the chief of staff, deputy chief of staff, legal counsel, press secretary, legislative director, and director of constituent service. Beyond the personal staff, the governor in Connecticut appoints thirty-seven commissioners, all of whom require legislative confirmation, and approximately 1,800 individuals to serve on numerous boards, commissions, and committees.[3] The Connecticut governor therefore has considerable appointment power, which in turn allows the governor to exercise control over executive branch activity. If needed, the governor can issue executive orders to subordinates that provide detailed instructions and guidelines for the execution of laws.

The Connecticut Constitution also identifies the governor as the "captain of the state militia." In conjunction with this quasi-military role, the governor has authority over the Connecticut National Guard. The Guard can be deployed by the governor to assist the state during times of natural disasters, such as devastating hurricanes and floods. The governor can also mobilize the National Guard in the interest of preserving law and order. However, should the Guard be needed to bolster the regular army during time of war or national emergency, the president of the United States can federalize the National Guard and deploy units according to the national interest. Thus, while the governor can direct the Guard to perform a variety of state-wide functions, the National Guard is ultimately under the jurisdiction of the president. The governor's military power is therefore subject to limitations. The deployment of Connecticut National Guard units to Iraq in recent years is an example of how the Guard can be federalized.

A quasi-judicial role is also afforded to the governor by the state constitution. The governor has the sole authority to grant a reprieve to persons after they have been convicted of a crime. According to the state constitution, a reprieve issued by the governor is valid only "until the end of the next session of the general assembly, and no longer." Gubernatorial reprieves in Connecticut are thus a temporary and somewhat short-lived respite from punishment. The power to grant reprieves is seldom exercised by the governor.

A ceremonial role for the state governor is not explicit in the state constitution, although such duty is most certainly implied in Article IV. In this regard, the governor is expected to engage in a wide range of symbolic activity, which includes cutting ribbons and making speeches at the opening of new schools, bridges, and highways. The governor is also expected to participate in Memorial Day parades, issue proclamations during state or federal holidays, attend the funerals of political dignitaries, and meet with student field trips to the state Capitol. Public image, poise, and style are important to the performance of ceremonial duties.

Like the president of the United States, the governor of Connecticut is expected to participate in several tasks not designated by the state constitution. Perhaps the most important task in this respect is that of party chief. It is expected that in addition to performing several constitutional duties, the governor should devote time and energy to promoting the goals and objectives of his or her political party. As party chief, the governor appoints the chairperson of the party's state central committee. The governor is also expected to raise funds for the party, appoint party loyalists to several administrative posts and judgeships, and campaign for the party's candidates during state, and local elections. Although no governor can possibly perform every duty with an equal amount of vigor and skill, it is reasonable to expect occupants of the governor's office to be flexible and multi-talented individuals.

Much to the advantage of the Connecticut governorship is the absence of term limitations in the state constitution. The Connecticut Constitution does not impose term limits on the office of governor, which tends to protect a governor from becoming a "lame duck." This of course is to the advantage of the governor, as state lawmakers often perceive an outgoing governor as "old news" and somewhat powerless. Hence there is less incentive on the part of lawmakers to support an outgoing governor's legislative agenda. In the absence of term limits, the governor can thus maintain political leverage throughout his or her term of office.[4]

Job Approval Ratings

Although a deep reservoir of constitutional power is to the advantage of a state governor, no governor can depend on constitutional power alone to effectively lead a state. Equally, if not more, important is the extent to which a governor can cultivate a high level of support from among the state's population. A governor's popularity among the general electorate is a critical source of power, particularly for those governors with an aggressive legislative agenda.[5]

Governors, like presidents, depend on popular support to exercise legislative leadership. State lawmakers are more inclined to support the legislative agenda of a governor with high job approval ratings, as opposed to one who has little support or respect among the general public. High job approval ratings are therefore essential to working effectively with the General Assembly. A state governor might very well be afforded a broad set of constitutional powers, but in the absence of high job approval ratings such authority is for all intents and purposes diminished. High approval ratings are especially important to those governors who do not enjoy the luxury of a partisan majority in the state legislature.

At the time of this writing, Governor M. Jodi Rell's job approval ratings have consistently hovered above 70 percent,[6] the highest approval ratings sustained by any Connecticut governor during the past twenty-five years.[7] The governor's unprecedented approval ratings are the principal reason why she has had a successful working relationship with a Democratic-controlled state legislature. A generally healthy state economy, an unemployment rate slightly below the national average, an express commitment on the governor's part to restoring ethics in government, an image of confident, but not arrogant, leadership, a down-to-earth personality, along with the support of popular issues in Connecticut, such as civil unions, the right to abortion, stem cell research, and campaign finance reform, are among the key reasons why Governor Rell, a Republican, has enjoyed such extraordinary approval ratings.

The State Judiciary

Article Five of the Connecticut Constitution establishes the state's judicial system. Over the years, the structure of the state's judicial system has been reorganized and streamlined into what is now a unified and efficient system of courts. The state's judicial system is professionally administered and staffed. Courts in Connecticut perform a vital role, and since the Constitution of 1818 the judiciary has functioned as an independent and equal branch of state government. Like the legislative and executive branches of government, it is apparent that the state judicial system has also been modernized and equipped to confront the challenges of the twenty-first century.

Superior Courts

Any discussion of Connecticut's judicial structure must begin with the state superior courts. These are the courts located at the base of the judicial system. Superior courts are trial courts of original jurisdiction. Superior courts are located throughout the state, and it is within the superior courts that the vast majority of day-to-day and routine judicial activity takes place. Superior courts are truly the "workhorses" of Connecticut's judicial system. In 2006, the superior court division included 13 judicial districts, 20 geographical areas, and 13 juvenile districts. A total of 179 superior court judges were working at this level of the state's judicial system.[8]

As a result of recent court reform efforts, superior courts are subdivided into five divisions, with cases processed into one of the five divisions depending on the class of the case.[9] The Civil Division of superior court is where personal disputes are resolved. Lawsuits that seek monetary compensation are often the subject of civil cases. Insurance claims resulting from automobile or motorcycle accidents, claims regarding contract violations, charges of libel and slander, and claims concerning faulty appliances or purchased goods are typical of cases routinely heard in the Civil Division of superior court. A jury can be impaneled in civil court, or the case can be decided by the judge assigned to the case. In Connecticut, as in other states, financial settlements are normally reached before the case is formally tried.

The Criminal Division of the superior court system is where individuals are prosecuted for committing crimes against the state of Connecticut. Punishment in criminal cases can range from community service or probation to a lengthy prison sentence. In a murder case, the person convicted can be sentenced to life in prison without parole or even sentenced to death. At the time of this writing, five individuals in Connecticut are awaiting execution on death row. In 2004, Connecticut executed convicted serial killer and rapist Michael Ross by lethal injection after Ross waived his rights to further appeal. This was the first execution in Connecticut since 1960, when "Mad Dog" Joseph Taborsky was executed by electric chair for his murder of package store clerks. Connecticut is one of thirty-eight states that still provides for the death penalty.

Assault with a deadly weapon, murder, grand theft, drug possession, arson, sale of liquor to a minor, and drunken driving are examples of cases heard in criminal court. As in civil cases, a jury can be impaneled or a case can be tried before a judge. Like other states, plea bargaining is very common in Connecticut with the vast majority of criminal cases resolved in this manner.

The Family Division of superior court resolves conflicts involving divorce, alimony, and child custody disputes, while the Juvenile Division handles cases involving young persons who are accused of a crime. In Connecticut, a "child" is defined as a person under the age of sixteen, while a "youth" is defined as an individual sixteen to eighteen years of age. Cases involving children and, in most instances, youths are heard in juvenile court. Court records involving juveniles are kept confidential and juvenile cases are not open to the public.[10]

The Housing Division of superior court decides cases concerning rental disputes that erupt between landlords and tenants. Although family, juvenile, and housing courts normally do not hear the most intriguing or publicized cases, such courts are nevertheless essential to the administration of justice within the state of Connecticut.

Intermediate Appellate Court

Decisions rendered in superior court are normally final and in most instances bring closure to a particular case. In some cases, however, one of the parties, either the defendant or plaintiff, might choose to appeal the jury's or judge's verdict. Should this occur, an appeal will be processed to the state's intermediate appellate court.

A special category of cases can be appealed directly from superior court to the state supreme court, although in most instances the case will first be appealed to the intermediate appellate court. In Connecticut, a person is normally granted one appeal.

Established in 1982 by Amendment XX of the state constitution, the intermediate appellate court was created to relieve the heavy and growing workload of the state supreme court. Prior to the establishment of the intermediate appellate court, cases would be appealed directly from state superior court to the state supreme court. Although the supreme court was under no obligation to grant a hearing to every appeal, the court's docket was nevertheless overcrowded. The intermediate court has thus served to reduce the workload of the supreme court, thereby allowing supreme court judges to concentrate on the most important and difficult judicial issues that arise in the state.

The intermediate appellate court, like the state supreme court, is located in Hartford. Nine judges are assigned to the intermediate court. One appellate judge, designated by the chief justice of the state supreme court, serves as the chief judge of the intermediate court. A three-judge panel normally hears an appeal, although in special cases the court will sit *en banc* (full bench; that is, all nine judges will hear the case).[11] A majority of judges on the appellate panel will decide whether or not to sustain the superior court verdict or reverse the lower court's judgment.

When a panel of judges is evaluating a case on appeal, the panel's primary concern is not with the facts of the case, nor with the guilt or innocence of the person appealing the case. The court instead is concerned with matters of law and constitutional procedure. The intermediate appellate court does not call witnesses, nor is a jury impaneled. The main concern is whether or not the lower court's decision was based on proper rules of constitutional procedure. Should a majority of the panel conclude that constitutional procedure was not followed, regardless of the facts, then the lower court's decision will most likely be reversed and either a new trial will be ordered or the case will be dismissed. Should the panel conclude that the lower court's decision was reached fairly and properly without constitutional infringement, then the judgment of the superior court will be sustained.

State Supreme Court

The court of last resort in Connecticut is normally the state supreme court. The supreme court hears cases that are appealed from the intermediate appellate court, and as previously noted, will hear a very select body of cases that are appealed directly from the superior courts. The Connecticut Supreme Court consists of seven judges, which includes six associate justices and the chief justice. Five justices will sit for a case, although in certain instances the chief justice will request that the court sit *en banc*. Like the intermediate appellate court, the state supreme court is not a trial court. There are no witnesses called to testify, there is no jury, and the justices are not particularly concerned with the facts of the case. Rules of evidence, constitutional procedure, and matters of law are what the state supreme court is primarily concerned with when hearing an appeal.

Cases arrive at the state supreme court in several different ways. One method is for an individual to appeal the ruling of the intermediate appellate court directly to the state supreme court. This is known as "petitioning for certification." Should two of the seven supreme court justices upon review of the petition decide that the appeal is worthy of a hearing, the court will grant the petition and request that all records of the case be forwarded to the court. With regard to petitions for certification, the supreme court has full discretion whether or not to grant the appeal.

The second way for a case to arrive before the supreme court is for the court to transfer a pending case that is before the intermediate appellate court. Any case filed in the intermediate appellate court can be directly transferred to the state supreme court upon the supreme court's request. A third route of appeal is for the decision of a superior court to be appealed directly to the state supreme court. State law carefully identifies which body of cases can be appealed directly to the state supreme court. Such cases include rulings involving the death penalty, legislative reapportionment, or those in which interpretation of the state constitution is required.[12]

When a case is brought before the state supreme court, there is a well-established system of procedure that unfolds. Lawyers for both sides of the case are allowed to argue their positions before the court. Both parties are allowed a half-hour for "oral argument." The court hears oral arguments during eight two-week sessions between the months of September and June of each year. The supreme court listens to as many as three or four cases during days scheduled for oral argument. During oral argument, the justices ask the lawyers representing the two parties a wide range of probing questions pertaining to judicial precedent and matters of law. Lawyers for both sides are expected to be well-prepared for oral argument and ready to field difficult questions from the sitting justices.

Following oral argument, the justices meet in the conference room located within the supreme court building to discuss the case. A preliminary vote is taken during the conference. One of the justices who is in the majority will be asked to draft a "majority opinion." Writing the court's majority opinion can be a difficult and delicate task, as the final opinion must be deemed acceptable to those justices who originally voted with the majority.

One or more of the justices who voted with the minority might feel compelled to draft a dissenting opinion, although this is not a formal requirement. A dissenting opinion reflects points of disagreement with the court's majority. Moreover, in addition to majority and dissenting opinions, one or more of the justices who voted with the majority might decide to draft a concurring opinion. A concurring opinion will be written by a justice who agrees with the majority's position with respect to the outcome of the case, but not necessarily with the specific reasons expressed in the majority opinion. One of the justices in the majority might agree with the majority view that a statute passed by the Connecticut state legislature is in violation of the Connecticut Constitution and should therefore be deemed unconstitutional. At the same time, however, the justice might not agree with the reasons expressed in the majority opinion regarding the invalidation of the law. In this instance, the justice may write a concurring opinion.

Drafts of majority, dissenting, and concurring opinions are circulated to the justices involved in the case. The justices will carefully read the drafts and evaluate the legal arguments. After the opinions have been circulated, read, and digested, the justices will meet once again in the conference room to cast their final vote. It is possible, but not probable, that a member of the majority might have been so impressed with the logic of the dissenting opinion that he or she will part company with the majority and affix his or her name to the dissenting opinion. Conversely, a justice who originally sided with the minority might be pulled to the side of the majority as a result of a compelling and persuasive majority opinion. Only after the separate opinions are drafted and reviewed does the position of the supreme court solidify. When supreme court rulings are issued, they are immediately made public by way of the Electronic Bulletin Board. Shortly thereafter, the decision is printed in the *Connecticut Law Journal*.[13]

Table Five documents the workload of the Connecticut Supreme Court during two recent terms.

Table 5
Supreme Court Caseload
July 1, 2002 – June 30, 2003

	Civil	Criminal	Total
Caseload	291	169	460
Appeals Disposed	135	63	198

July 1, 2003 – June 30, 2004			
	Civil	Criminal	Total
Caseload	296	168	464
Appeals Disposed	161	76	237

Source: Biennial Report of the Connecticut Judicial Branch: http://www.jud.ct.gov/Publications/BiennialStats2002-04.pdf.

As the data show, the state supreme court's yearly docket currently consists of approximately 460 cases. This figure includes fresh appeals as well as appeals carried over from the previous term. The data also show that the court will issue rulings for approximately 40-50 percent of the cases on the docket. In a typical term, approximately two-thirds of the rulings involve civil appeals.

The state supreme court is normally, but not always, the court of last resort. If a case involves interpretation of the federal constitution, the losing party has the right to appeal the case directly to the United States Supreme Court by petitioning the high court for a writ of *certiorari*. In essence, the party appealing the case is asking the Supreme Court to "make more certain" of the lower court ruling. It is doubtful, however, that the Supreme Court will agree to hear the case, as approximately 98 percent of petitions for *certiorari* are routinely denied.[14] Should the case involve interpretation of the state constitution, the decision of the state supreme court is final. As discussed in Chapter Three, the United States Supreme Court cannot review the ruling of a state supreme court regarding interpretation of the state constitution.

Judicial Selection

The judicial selection process in Connecticut was at one time a political and partisan process. The governor would nominate judges and the state legislature would confirm or reject the governor's choice. Judicial posts were part of the patronage system, with party affiliation and political loyalty at the heart of the selection process. The judicial selection process in Connecticut was very similar to that of the federal judicial selection process.

Connecticut's judicial selection system underwent significant reform in 1986 with passage of the Twenty-Fifth Amendment to the state constitution. Passage of the Twenty-Fifth Amendment reflected a national trend regarding court reform at the state level of the federal system. In many states, the process of judicial selection had theoretically been depoliticized, reflecting the public's antipathy toward politics, patronage, and political parties. Reform proposals were adopted across the land that placed greater emphasis on the merit of judicial nominees as opposed to partisanship and political connections.

The roots of the reform effort can be traced to Missouri's pioneering efforts in 1940 regarding state judicial selection procedures. The "Missouri Plan" established a system that incorporated a mixture of merit and gubernatorial involvement, as well as popular referendum in the selection of state judges.[15] A number of states, Connecticut included, have since followed the lead of Missouri by either adopting the Missouri Plan in its entirety or certain elements of the system.

The Twenty-Fifth amendment to the Connecticut Constitution established a Judicial Selection Commission for the purpose of developing a short-list of potential judicial nominees. The Selection Commission is required to review and evaluate the credentials of lawyers and sitting judges who have expressed an interest in serving on either the superior, appellate, or state supreme court. The Commission will narrow the list of qualified candidates to three or four and present the list to the governor. The governor will then select a candidate from the Commission's short-list and forward the name to the state legislature for confirmation.

The process in the state legislature begins with hearings in the Judiciary Committee, which is one of the standing committees in the General Assembly. The hearings are followed by a Committee vote. Should the Judiciary Committee recommend the nominee, the state legislature will then vote to confirm or reject the candidate. Judges in Connecticut must have earned a law degree and be a member of the Connecticut bar. Superior, appellate, and supreme court judges are appointed to eight year terms and are eligible for reappointment. State judges must retire at the age of seventy, although judges seventy or older can serve as state referees.

The screening of judicial candidates by the Judicial Selection Commission and the development of a short-list based on merit is an important departure from the previous system of judicial selection. Under the current system, the governor still has some discretion in deciding which name to send to the legislature for confirmation, but is formally obligated to nominate a judge from among the list of candidates proposed by the Commission. The governor's role in the selection of state judges has been somewhat, but by no means entirely, diminished.

The Judicial Selection Commission is a twelve-member bipartisan commission. The Commission is at all times politically balanced, with equal numbers of Democrats and Republicans. Among the twelve Commission members, six are lawyers appointed by the governor and six are persons outside of the legal profession appointed by party leaders within the state House and state Senate. More specifically, the Speaker of the House appoints two members, the Senate pro tempore appoints two, and the minority leaders in both chambers each appoint one. Commission members are appointed for six years.[16]

It would of course be naive to think that all politics has been removed from the judicial selection process in Connecticut as a result of the Twenty-Fifth amendment and the creation of the Judicial Selection Commission. Moreover, there is very little evidence to suggest that state judges in Connecticut since 1986 have been more competent, meritorious, and objective than judges chosen under the former selection process. The current procedure for appointing Commission members inherently lends itself to political favoritism, and Commission members undoubtedly have strong political opinions about legal issues. Moreover, those individuals recommended by the Commission and eventually appointed to the bench have often been involved in one form or another in state or local politics. It is important to note in this regard that comparative studies of state judicial recruitment have concluded that different selection methods do not alter the characteristics and quality of judges.[17] State judges are strikingly similar to one another, regardless of which judicial selection system is in place.

Judicial Support Staffs

Like state lawmakers and the state governor, judges in Connecticut depend on a number of support personnel to assist with the day-to-day operation of the judicial system. Support personnel range from law clerks and high-level judicial administrators to clerical personnel who process forms and file documents.

Law clerks are central to the functioning of the state's judicial system. Fourteen law clerks currently serve the state supreme court. Law clerks are selected by the individual justices and serve for a period of twelve months. Law clerks are normally fresh out of law school and are in the top tier of their graduating class. The job description for a state supreme court law clerk suggests that an applicant be among the top quarter of his or her graduating class. In Connecticut, as in other states, it is considered an honor to serve as a law clerk for the state supreme court. The position is also perceived as a stepping stone for a successful career in law. Needless to say, the selection process is highly competitive. Law clerks perform a number of critical functions. These include helping justices screen and review petitions for certification, researching legal precedents, preparing justices for oral argument, and writing and editing drafts of judicial opinions.

Eighteen law clerks are assigned to the intermediate court of appeals. Like law clerks for the state supreme court, such individuals are screened and personally selected by the individual appellate court judges. Several of the law clerks also work as "shared clerks" for the court and for retired appellate court judges. The functions of law clerks who serve the intermediate appellate court are very similar to those of supreme court law clerks. Screening cases, researching precedent, preparing judges for oral argument and assisting with opinions are among the normal duties of appellate court law clerks. Appellate court law clerks are expected to be among the top third of their law school graduating class.[18]

Law clerks are also hired to serve the needs of the state's superior courts. Superior court law clerks are not personally chosen by superior court judges, but rather are assigned to various superior courts based on the needs of superior court judges. Such law clerks assist judges by performing tasks similar to those of law clerks working in the intermediate appellate court and the state supreme court. Assistance with opinion writing and legal research are among the principal duties associated with being a superior court clerk. Superior court law clerks are hired for twelve months, and while class standing is considered relevant to the hiring process, no specific tier is designated in the job posting.[19] In addition to law clerks, the Connecticut judicial system is supported by several administrative divisions that fall under the direction of the chief court administrator. The various administrative divisions are responsible for managing the state judicial system and for implementing the decisions of the courts. The Administrative Services Division is responsible for managing judicial facilities, processing data, and handling personnel matters. The Affirmative Action/Employment Discrimination Division is responsible for ensuring that citizens have equal access to the courts and that affirmative action guidelines are followed with respect to staffing the administrative components of the judiciary. The Court Support Services Division includes the Office of Adult Probation, Office of Alternative Sanctions, Bail Commission, Family Services Division, and the Division of Juvenile Detention Services. The various components of the Court Support Services Division work very closely with superior courts regarding terms of probation, rehabilitation programs, bail requirements, and issues involving family relationships and juvenile delinquency.

The public arm of the state's judicial system is the External Affairs Division, which is responsible for educating the public through programs regarding the structure and function of the judicial system. The Superior Court Operations Division includes a wide range of subdivisions responsible for implementing court rulings, providing legal services to superior court judges, and for ensuring ethical conduct on the part of attorneys who practice law in Connecticut.[20]

Generally speaking, many offices and divisions have been established for the purpose of processing judicial cases, implementing judicial rulings and helping judges with the task of deciding cases and issuing opinions. Approximately 4,000 full and part-time employees work in various capacities within the judicial branch of government.[21] While on paper elements of the judicial administrative structure might appear unnecessary, there can be little doubt that the administrative components of the state judicial system have in multiple ways helped, rather than hindered, the efficiency of the judiciary. In many states, the judicial system seems to lag far behind that of the legislative and executive branches of government with regard to efficiency, modernization, staffing, and support services. This does not appear to be the case in Connecticut. The recent reorganization of the state superior court system, the addition of an intermediate court of appeals, the establishment of the Judicial Selection Commission, along with the addition of staff personnel and support services clearly suggest a judicial branch of government well prepared to face the many unexpected and multidimensional legal challenges of the future.

Notes

1. Kevin B. Smith, Alan Greenblatt, and John Buntin, with Charles S. Clark, *Governing States and Localities* (Washington: Congressional Quarterly Press, 2005), pp. 215-16.

2. Louis W. Koenig, *The Chief Executive*, 5th ed. (New York: Harcourt Brace Jovanovich, 1986), p. 386.

3. Information on Governor Rell's staff was obtained from a phone conversation with the governor's office, while numbers for commissions and boards was obtained from the Secretary of State's website, www.sots.ct.gov/Capitol/BdsComms/GetAppointed.htm.

4. Connecticut's governorship is ranked 3.8 on a scale that ranges from 2.7 to 4.1, which places the office among the stronger gubernatorial offices in the U.S. Seven measures are utilized to evaluate the power of a particular governorship, including, among others, term of office, the ability to appoint and remove executive officials and the scope of veto power. See Thad Beyle, "The Governors," in Virginia Gray and Russell Hanson, eds., *Politics in the American States: A Comparative Analysis*, 8th ed. (Washington: Congressional Quarterly Press, 2003). Data adapted and presented in Ann O'M. Bowman and Richard C. Kearney, *State and Local Government*, 3rd ed. (Boston: Houghton Mifflin, 2006), p. 160, Table 7.3.

5. The centrality of public support for effective legislative leadership is discussed in several works on state politics. See, for example, Dye and MacManus, *Politics in States and Communities*, pp. 255, 258; and Smith, Greenblatt, and Buntin, with Clark, *Governing States and Localities*, p. 233.

6. Quinnipiac University Poll, released August 17, 2006, online at www.quinnipiac.edu/x11362.xml?ReleaseID=948.

7. Collapsing the excellent and good categories, Governor William O'Neill's public approval rating from 1981-90 averaged approximately 38 percent, Governor Lowell P. Weicker, Jr.'s average approval rating from 1991-94 was approximately 36 percent, while Governor Rowland's public approval rating from 1995 to 2004 averaged approximately 46 percent. University of Connecticut Center for Survey Research and Analysis, online at www.csra.uconn.edu/pdf/Courant.

8. "Fast Facts about the Judicial Branch," online at www.jud.ct.gov/external/media/facts.htm.

9. *Searching for Justice: Connecticut's Courts* (Hartford: Connecticut Judicial Department, 1990), p. 12.

10. *Searching for Justice*, p. 23.

11. *Connecticut's Courts* (Hartford: State of Connecticut Judicial Branch), p. 14.

12. *Searching for Justice*, p. 25; *Connecticut's Courts*, p. 12; "Judicial Branch," online at www.jud.state.ct.us/external/supapp/casecome.html.

13. "Judicial Branch," online at www.jud.state.ct.us/external/supapp/aro.htm.

14. Henry R. Glick, *Courts, Politics, and Justice*, 3rd ed. (New York: McGraw Hill, Inc. 1993), p. 277.

15. The "Missouri Plan" works as follows: A nominating commission produces a short-list of prospective judges to the state governor. Merit is the principal consideration in the development of the short-list and the governor is required to appoint a judge from the names recommended by the commission. After a minimum of one year, the electorate votes to either retain or remove the judge. The popular referendum coincides with a general election and the issue of judicial retention appears on the election ballot. The Missouri Plan, also known as the Merit Plan, combines the work of a bipartisan nominating commission, gubernatorial appointment, and popular referendum. A review of the different state judicial selection procedures can be found in Glick, *Courts, Politics, and Justice*, pp. 116-26.

16. *Connecticut Law Tribune*, December 15, 1986.

17. Glick, *Courts, Politics, and Justice*, pp. 131-33.

18. "Judicial Branch," online at www.jud.state.ct.us./external/supapp/lawclerkapp.html.

19. "Judicial Branch," online at www.jud.state.ct.us./external/super/superiorclerk.html.

20. "Judicial Branch," online at www.jud.state.ct.us./ystday/adminop.html.

21. Full-time employees including judges is recorded at 3,968 and permanent part-time employees at 121. Data obtained from phone conversation with Human Services Management Unit of the Judicial Branch, October 12, 2006.

CHAPTER SEVEN

Connecticut's Watchdogs

The role of media in covering Connecticut politics was not one of the topics in the first edition of this book. This was not due to a lack of respect for the media on the part of the author. Instead, at the time the first edition was written it seemed as if the media were essentially reporting and describing developments in Connecticut politics, rather than aggressively investigating what issues were behind or beneath reported stories. However, between the writing of the first and second editions, a period of approximately six years, the media in Connecticut appeared to assume a new and quite different role in their coverage of Connecticut politics. "Investigative journalism," a term associated with reporters such as Bob Woodward and Carl Bernstein of the *Washington Post*, now seemed to characterize the reporting of several media outlets in Connecticut. Unearthing and exposing political scandals now became a fairly common activity for political reporters in Connecticut, with newspapers in particular at the forefront of this intriguing development.

Much to their credit, newspapers, more than any other information source in the state of Connecticut, appear to be serving as the true "watchdogs" over Connecticut's political system. Thus, it would be remiss for a fresh text on Connecticut government not to devote a chapter to the challenging tasks and noble efforts of those individuals known as investigative journalists. Quite frankly, were it not for the work of investigative newspaper journalists employed by local newspapers, deceitful and corrupt public officials, several of whom have wielded extraordinary power at the state and local level government, would continue to degrade and blemish Connecticut's long tradition of good government.

Newspapers

Although the raw number of newspapers as well as the percentage of persons who read newspapers have severely declined in states across the land, due primarily to the advent of television as a news source, there are still several daily newspapers published in Connecticut that provide readers with an in-depth and substantive look at state and local politics.[1] Among the two hundred newspapers with the widest circulation in the United States, four are based in Connecticut. The *Hartford Courant,* which proudly claims credit on its front page as "America's Oldest Continuously Published Newspaper" has a Sunday circulation of 272,919. The *New Haven Register*'s Sunday circulation is 90,389, followed by The *Connecticut Post*'s Sunday circulation at 85,772. The fourth largest circulation belongs to The *Waterbury American-Republican* with a Sunday circulation of 61,100.[2]

In addition to the four newspapers with the widest circulation, a number of newspapers in Connecticut with a more limited circulation also devote considerable space to politics and government. The *Danbury News Times*, Meriden's *Record Journal*, the *Norwalk Hour* ,and the *Stamford Advocate* are examples of such informative and politically penetrating publications. Currently, there are a total of sixty-nine newspapers with varying degrees of circulation published in Connecticut, along with a variety of creative and captivating campus newspapers. There is certainly no shortage of print press in the state of Connecticut. For those who prefer reading a newspaper online, practically all of the newspapers in Connecticut can be read on the Internet. The information one reads is identical to hard copy, although the reader will have to contend with a plethora of advertisements and pop-ups interspersed in the body of articles.

Television and Radio Stations

Television and radio stations are also present in Connecticut and provide the citizenry with yet another source of political information, albeit less substantive than stories in the print press. The ABC (Channel 8, New Haven) CBS (Channel 3, Hartford) NBC (Channel 30, Hartford) and Fox (Channel 61, Hartford) affiliates employ political reporters and routinely provide informative and easily digestible political newscasts on a daily basis. Cablevision 12 in Norwalk also devotes a considerable amount of time to Connecticut politics, despite a regional audience confined to a portion of New York state and Fairfield County in Connecticut.

For those who prefer to watch their government in action without narration, cable channel CT-N is ideal for this purpose. This is Connecticut's equivalent of C-Span. Committee hearings at the state Capitol in Hartford, reports from commissioners, speeches by the governor, and a variety of activity on the floors of the General Assembly are available for uninterrupted viewing on CT-N.

FM and AM radio stations located in Connecticut also provide a degree of coverage concerning unfolding political events in Connecticut. The stations vary in their attention to political stories, but one can find several that probe the political landscape in considerable depth. AM stations such as WELI (960 AM), WICC (600 AM), and WTIC (1080 AM) do a good job of covering state and local politics, while the National Public Radio affiliates, WEDW (88 FM), WNPR (89.1), and WSHU (91.1) are clearly the best in terms of detailed reporting and commentary concerning the Connecticut political scene. There are currently 101 radio stations located in the state of Connecticut.[3]

Blogs

For those who prefer non-traditional and purely citizen-based political reporting, the blogosphere offers yet another medium for political news. Politically-oriented blogs are often created by citizens to promote a particular point of view regarding candidates and political issues, although some blogs are created for the purpose of facilitating political dialogue and discussion. Although blogs (short for web logs) should not be viewed in the same light as newspapers and other forms of journalism, they do serve to inform citizens about important developments within government and the political arena. Young political activists in particular are the most familiar with and attracted to blogs. Indeed, many seem to depend on blogs for their daily political information and perhaps even voting cues. The political impact of blogs with regard to shaping political information as well as the motivations of those who create and maintain blogs, i.e., the "bloggers," calls for extended research and analysis.

There are currently 57 million blogs on the web, with 1.3 million posts recorded each day and 54,000 posts recorded per hour.[4] Among the 57 million blogs, however, it is estimated that only 55 percent can be classified as "active" blogs. Blogs have become a global phenomenon, and appear in many different languages as well, most notably English and Japanese.[5] Not all blogs are political and one can find blogs devoted to an extraordinary array of subjects well beyond that of politics. Nevertheless, the political "blogosphere" is what has attracted the most attention.

Blogs made their debut in American politics during the emotionally charged presidential campaign of the former Democratic governor of Vermont, Howard Dean. Although Dean failed in his bid to win the Democratic Party's presidential nomination, blogs continued to proliferate across the land. As noted in Chapter Three, blogs were credited with propelling the 2006 Connecticut senate campaign of insurgent Democratic challenger Ned Lamont. The blogosphere was often cited by pundits as one of the contributing factors behind Lamont's primary victory against Senator Joe Lieberman. During the 2006 general election, bloggers both inside and outside the state devoted a great deal of their energy to supporting Lamont and other Democratic candidates in hotly contested Connecticut races.

In addition to campaign reporting in newspapers such as the *Hartford Courant* and *Connecticut Post,* one could follow campaign developments on a daily basis by reading Connecticut-based and non-Connecticut-based blogs. In the state, for example, Connecticut Bob, My Left Nutmeg, Connecticut Blue, and Cup of Joe were exceptionally active with regard to posting comments and views concerning Connecticut election contests. The extent to which the traditional media trolled blogs looking for leads and late breaking developments in campaigns is difficult to assess, although there is reason to believe that newspaper reporters scanned blogs with some regularity, searching for fresh information and leads. Regardless of how one perceives the information value of blogs, the fact of the matter is that an increasing number of citizens are receiving political information from this Internet phenomenon. Any person can create a blog at virtually no cost.

Investigative Journalism: A Challenging Task

Working as an investigative journalist for a newspaper is not an easy task in this day and age. Although a large majority of Americans support the media's role as a watchdog over the political process, many Americans are nevertheless skeptical of the media's motivations. In a 2001 survey of 1,012 adults conducted by the Center for Survey Research and Analysis housed at the University of Connecticut, 82 percent of citizens surveyed indicated that it was important for the media to watch over government. At the same time, however, 71 percent of persons surveyed believed that it was desirable for the government to hold the media in check.[6] When asked if they were more concerned with the freedom afforded to the media or government censorship of the press, 41 percent of the respondents expressed concern with the former, while only 36 percent indicated a concern with the latter. Moreover, 46 percent of respondents in the survey stated that the press has been allowed "too much freedom."[7]

The survey data presented above are not the only reason why working as an investigative journalist is a daunting profession in this day and age. Additionally, newspapers across the country are currently downsizing their journalistic staffs, which further impedes investigative efforts.[8] According to Howard Kurtz, a respected staff writer for the *Washington Post*, declining revenues resulting from a decrease in newspaper circulation appear to be the basis for such an unfortunate development. Moreover, a desire on the part of corporate CEOs to maximize profits has further contributed to staff downsizing. Examples of downsizing cited by Kurtz include the *Dallas Morning News* and *Cleveland Plain Dealer*, two major newspapers that suffered severe staff cutbacks of 19 and 17 percent respectively. The newsroom staff of the *Philadelphia Inquirer* was also trimmed by 15 percent, while 8 percent of the newsroom staff at the *Washington Post* accepted early retirement packages. The cutbacks, according to Kurtz, will inevitably result in "fewer bodies to pore over records at City Hall, the statehouse or federal agencies."[9] How newspapers can generate future revenue and hire staff writers to cover politics and government are clearly among the serious challenges facing the newspaper industry in the twenty-first century. The continued staff cutbacks and loss in revenue, according to Kurtz, are "bad news for serious journalism, and good news for corrupt politicians."[10]

However, irrespective of cutbacks in the number of investigative journalists employed by newspapers along with public skepticism towards media reporting, the print press in the state of Connecticut has still been able to investigate and report the malfeasance of public officials in great detail and with amazing persistence. Newspaper revelations of illegal activity involving the mayor's office in the city of Bridgeport, as well as in the office of state governor, demonstrate quite clearly that investigative journalism is alive and well in the Constitution State.

The Ganim and Rowland Scandals

The reporting of the *Connecticut Post* regarding the scandalous activity of Bridgeport Mayor Joseph P. Ganim, as well as the investigative reporting of the *Hartford Courant* concerning the illegal activity of Governor John G. Rowland were journalistic efforts worthy of a Pulitzer Prize. The investigative reporting of both newspapers underscores why a free, fierce, and unbridled press is essential to the preservation of the American republic.

It is not the intention of this chapter to chronicle the investigative reporting of the *Connecticut Post* that resulted in the federal conviction and imprisonment of Bridgeport Mayor Ganim. Nor is there any need to review in detail the investigative work of the *Hartford Courant*, which led to Governor Rowland's resignation from office and federal imprisonment. For those interested in the sordid details of the two separate scandals, the archives of both the *Post* and the *Courant* should provide a treasure-trove of information. Suffice it to say, investigative journalists for both newspapers were able to assemble a puzzle – piece-by-piece and day-by-day – that depicted a pattern of greed, deceit, preferential public contracts, various forms of bribery, and sinister cabals of so-called "public servants" who used their power in ways that not only broke the law but also violated the public's trust. Although some might argue that both newspapers piggybacked on the work of federal investigators, the sequence of events which led to the downfall of Mayor Ganim and Governor Rowland suggested that the *Post* and *Courant* reporters were the first to unearth their scandalous activity. The tireless work of reporters is what provided federal agents with the signposts necessary for an effective investigation.

After a lengthy trial in federal district court, Mayor Ganim was found guilty under sixteen separate counts, including, among others, tax evasion and racketeering. The five-term Democratic mayor and former candidate for lieutenant governor, who had been mentioned quite often as a possible gubernatorial candidate, was sentenced to nine years in federal prison. Associates of Ganim were also convicted and received prison sentences that varied in length. For those who closely watched the Ganim scandal unfold, it was clear that the investigative reporting and coordination of reporting on the part of Bill Cummings of the *Connecticut Post* was primarily responsible for Ganim's downfall. Cummings's reports and journalistic queries always seemed to be one step ahead of the F.B.I.'s undercover investigation. A veteran and seasoned journalist, Cummings is known for his objective, thorough, and

uncompromising reports concerning government corruption in the
city of Bridgeport. Cummings described his work as an investigative
journalist in these terms:

> When people ask me what I do for a living I usually tell
> them that I'm a government cop. I'm the guy who asks
> what government is doing and why. It's not always easy, and
> government does not like to reveal its secrets. But the clues
> are there if you look, in the piles of documents and paper
> that government generates. Those are a reporter's tools,
> along with the sources who offer information. I checked
> out dozens and dozens of tips during the Ganim
> investigation. Many went nowhere. Others were right on
> the mark. It can be a tedious and time-consuming process,
> but that's the way it goes. You keep digging and sooner or
> later the truth, or at least a version close to it, emerges.[11]

Unlike Ganim, who chose to face a federal trial, Governor Rowland
agreed to plead guilty to the minor federal criminal charge of
depriving the state of Connecticut of honest services. Rowland, a
Republican who had recently been elected to the state governorship
for an unprecedented third term, was sentenced to one year and one
day in federal prison followed by four months of house arrest.
Although the work of federal investigators was central to Rowland's
demise, it was more than evident that investigative journalists
employed by the *Hartford Courant* were the individuals unearthing
and exposing the governor's illegal actions. Like the *Connecticut
Post's* investigation of Mayor Ganim, stories published by the
Courant seemed to structure the federal investigation. David
Altimari, one of the two lead investigative journalists for the
Courant during the entire Rowland episode, described the
relationship between the stories published by the *Courant* and the
investigative activity of federal agents as follows: "The stories led
federal investigators, who seemed reluctant to go after Rowland, to
start an investigation of the governor, and ultimately he plead guilty
in federal court. None of it would have happened without the

Courant's stories exposing Rowland using the power of his office for personal gain."[12] Members of Rowland's administration and close associates involved in the sandal were also convicted of various crimes and received prison sentences.

The Spirit of Jefferson

Generally speaking, the investigative work of the *Connecticut Post* and *Hartford Courant* provides special meaning to the perspective of Thomas Jefferson, one of our nation's foremost Founding Fathers and a staunch advocate of a free press. Writing to Archibald Stuart in 1799, Jefferson had this to say concerning a free press: "Our citizens may be deceived for a while, and have been deceived; but as long as the presses can be protected, we may trust to them for light."[13] Much to their credit and much to the benefit of the Connecticut citizenry, the *Connecticut Post* and the *Hartford Courant* have served as sources of "light" in their reporting of political corruption at both the local and state level of government. The thoughtful words of Bill Cummings concisely summarize the critical importance of objective and aggressive investigative journalism: "Reporters don't set policy; we examine it. We have no special license or privilege. But without people who are willing to poke and probe, democracy does not work. It will only benefit those in power."[14] For those who care about the exercise of political power, and who believe that ethics and good government are inseparable, it should be gratifying to know that there are still individuals employed by newspapers who keep a watchful eye over the conduct of government and who report corruption when they see it. Thomas Jefferson would most certainly applaud the efforts of Connecticut's watchdogs.

Notes

1. See "The State of the News Media 2004: An Annual Report on American Journalism," online at www.stateofthenewsmedia.org/narrative_ newspapers_audience.asp?cat. The report notes that slightly more than half

(54 percent) of Americans read a daily newspaper, while 62 percent read a Sunday edition. Moreover, the number of newspapers in the U.S. has declined by 1 percent each year for the past two decades.

2. ABC's FAS-FAX ending March 31, 2006, online at www.accessabc.com/reader/top150.htm.

3. Online at www.shgresources.com/ct/radio.

4. Dave Sifry, "State of the Blogosphere, October 2006," online at technorati.com/weblog/2006/11/161.html.

5. Sifry, "State of the Blogosphere, October 2006."

6. Kenneth A. Paulson, "Good News, Bad News in Latest First Amendment Survey," June 28, 2001, p. 1, online at www.freedomforum.org/templates/document.asp?documentID=14257.

7. Paulson, "Good News, Bad News," p. 2.

8. Howard Kurtz, "Reporters as Detectives," Washingtonpost.com, October 23, 2006, p. 2, online at www.washingtonpost.com/wp-dyn/content/blog/2006/10/23/BL2006102300297-pf.

9. Kurtz, "Reporters as Detectives," p. 2.

10. Kurtz, "Reporters as Detectives," p. 2.

11. Quotation obtained from Bill Cummings via e-mail, November 27, 2006.

12. Quotation obtained from David Altimari via e-mail, December 19, 2006.

13. Thomas Jefferson on Politics and Government," online at etext.virginia.edu/jeffersonquotations/Jeff1600.htm, p. 3.

14. Bill Cummings, November 27, 2006.

Conclusion

In his inaugural address delivered on the east side of the United States Capitol on January 20, 1961, President John F. Kennedy summoned the American people to the cause of public service. Kennedy's inaugural speech, regarded as one of the most thoughtful and dynamic inaugural speeches in the history of the United States, is especially remembered for one simple yet eloquent sentence. The newly-inaugurated, youthful, and charismatic president proclaimed: "And so my fellow Americans ask not what your country can do for you, ask what you can do for you country." Public service in Kennedy's view was a noble calling, and serving a cause greater than oneself was the mark of a patriot.

As a young boy, I personally witnessed JFK deliver a riveting speech on the New Haven town green during the highly competitive 1960 presidential contest Although I was raised in a politically active family, I truly believe that JFK's positive impact on American politics, as well as his short-lived presidency, contributed in several ways to my own interest in politics and government. There was something very special about President John F. Kennedy, which to this day continues to set him apart from other presidents and political figures.

In some respects, the spirit of JFK is present throughout the pages of this textbook. At the risk of sounding like an idealist, my intent in writing this work was not only to educate students concerning the mechanics and nuances of Connecticut government, but also to motivate college students to participate in the political process. I do not and will not subscribe to the view expressed by many cynical Americans that the political process is a closed system, open to only wealthy and powerful individuals. I will never surrender to this line of thinking as long as I teach political science. I contend instead that the political process, especially at the state and local level of government, is not only a porous process, but also in desperate need of young, educated, and ethical public servants. Put differently, the door to the political arena is open to those who wish to take advantage of it. Any person, irrespective of income, race, ethnicity, or religion, can directly participate in the political process and make an important contribution. Consider, for example, the four following excellent opportunities in the state of Connecticut for college students to participate in the affairs of government:

Elected Office: In Connecticut, a resident only has to be 18 years of age to run for a seat in the General Assembly. The same is true for a seat on a local town council, a local school board, or a local commission. The participation of young persons between the ages of 18-21 in the state legislature or in elected positions at the local level would not only enrich the quality of political discourse but also elevate the political voice of young adults. Imagine the extraordinary difference that a caucus of young persons could make in the Connecticut General Assembly, or perhaps on a town council. Think of the difference that young and perceptive lawmakers could make with respect to formulating Connecticut's $36 billion biennial budget. Or consider the impact young town councilors could make regarding a proposal to cut spending for the high school athletic program or the town's music curriculum. There are 151 seats in the Connecticut House of Representatives and 36 seats in the state Senate. Moreover, there are thousands of elected posts, ranging from council seats to commissions, in the 169 local communities across the state of Connecticut. Numerous opportunities exist therefore for young adults to hold public office and to make a serious difference in the policy process.

Party Politics: Young persons of college age can also influence the political process in ways other than holding elective office. For example, an individual who is 18 years of age or older can register with a political party and through the proper contacts become a member of a local town committee. Although the power of political parties has receded over the years, local party committees in Connecticut are still in many ways integral to the functioning of state and local politics. The local party organization is the ideal mechanism for persons who prefer to work behind the scenes. And let's not forget that membership on a town committee can also lead to an appointment on a local or state commission and eventually a nomination for public office. My own research and discussion with party leaders has discovered that many vacancies exist on local town committees. I have also learned that Democratic and Republican town chairpersons are very interested in having young and enthusiastic individuals join the town committees. Those who wish to participate in the political process would be wise to remember that membership on a local Democratic or Republican party committee is still the gateway into Connecticut politics. Although committees for third parties are not always present in local communities, opportunities do exist to participate in third-party movements. Like the Democratic and Republican parties in Connecticut, the Green Party, Libertarian Party, Concerned Citizens Party, and Working Families Party are all looking for young volunteers to advance their party's cause.

Interest Groups: Special and public interest groups are also in need of motivated and thoughtful activists. Joining an interest group and fighting for a particular interest can be an exhilarating political experience. Moreover, such activity will inevitably result in direct contact with state and local policy makers. Participation in an interest group can also lead to employment as a lobbyist at the Connecticut state Capitol. Although the term "lobbying" has a somewhat negative connotation in the minds of many Americans, the fact of the matter is that economic, social, and political interests need to be represented when lawmakers are passing a bill. Whether the interest represented is that of an insurance company, a labor union, or handicapped citizens, it is my contention that interest group activity and lobbying are valuable and noble forms of public service.

Voting: The most nominal yet vitally important way in which young persons can make a difference is through the simple act of voting. There is an election every year in Connecticut, for federal, state, or local public office. As in other states across the land, a person has to be only 18 years of age or older and a state resident to cast a vote on election day. Once again, imagine the extraordinary impact 18-21 years olds could make in both primary and general elections if they voted in large numbers. Unfortunately, voter turnout is distressingly low among young persons in this particular age bracket. Reasons given by young persons for not voting include a lack of information about candidates, registration difficulties, unfamiliarity with absentee voting procedures, negative perceptions towards politicians, time constraints, and a feeling that one vote doesn't make a difference, along with the attitude that "things never really change" regardless of which party wins an election. I take issue with many of the reasons, or excuses, expressed by students for not voting. I also stress to my students that election results do matter and that it does make a difference which political party controls the government. American foreign policy, spending priorities on the part of government, tax rates and tax cuts, interest rates, health insurance, environmental protection, and transportation policy, as well as the guidelines that regulate student loans for higher education are among the many policies directly affected by election outcomes. As I often tell my students, persons who do not vote are essentially allowing those who do vote to determine their future. Quite frankly, there are no longer any obstacles to voting in the United States. The property, race, gender, age, and residence barriers have all been lowered and practically any American citizen who is the resident of a state and has a home address can vote in a local, state, or federal election.

One of my favorite maxims, attributed to the English philosopher Sir Francis Bacon (1526-1626), states rather simply that "knowledge is power." This, in my view, is a very accurate statement, particularly as it applies to political power. Needless to say, it is virtually impossible for a person, or group of persons, to influence the course of government without first acquiring knowledge regarding the structure and mechanics of the political system. At the same time, however, I also believe that knowledge must be accompanied by political action. Indeed, a person can have a detailed working knowledge of the political system, but without political action such knowledge for all intents and purposes is inconsequential. Thus, I have written this introductory textbook with a dual purpose in mind. My intent was to not only increase the reader's knowledge of Connecticut government, but also to stimulate participation, *particularly on the part of college students*, in the political process. I sincerely hope that the readers of this text have acquired useful political knowledge, and as a result feel prepared to apply this knowledge within the political arena.

Select Bibliography:
Connecticut Politics, Government, and History

Collier, Christopher. "The Fundamental Orders of Connecticut and American Constitutionalism," *Connecticut Law Review* 21 (summer, 1989): 863-69.

_____. "Why Connecticut is 'The Constitution State,' " *Connecticut Bar Journal* 61 (1987): 210-14.

DeLong, Thomas A. *John Davis Lodge.* Fairfield, CT: Sacred Heart University Press, 1999.

Graham, Kenneth A. "Issues of Federalism in Connecticut in the Twentieth Century," *Connecticut History* 21 (November 1988): 116-29.

Grant, Ellsworth S. *The Miracle of Connecticut.* Hartford: Connecticut Historical Society, 1992.

Horton, Wesley W. *The Connecticut State Constitution: A Reference Guide.* Westport: Greenwood Press, 1993.

Lambert, Edward R. *History of New Haven Colony.* New Haven: Hitchcock and Stafford, 1838.

Lieberman, Joseph I. *The Power Broker.* Boston: Houghton and Mifflin, 1966.

_____. *The Legacy*. Hartford: Spoonwood Press, 1981.

Lockard, Duane. *New England State Politics*. Princeton: Princeton University Press, 1959.

McKee, Clyde D. Jr. "Connecticut: A Political System in Transition." In Josephine F. Milburn and William Doyle, eds., *New England Political Parties*. Cambridge: Schenkman Publishing Co., 1983.

Morehouse, Sarah M. and Malcolm E. Jewell. "Connecticut." In Andrew Apleton and Daniel S. Ward, eds., *State Party Profiles: a 50-State Guide to Development, Organization and Resources*. Washington: Congressional Quarterly, 1997.

Morse, Jarvis Means. *A Neglected Period of Connecticut History: 1818-1850*. New York: Octagon Books, 1978.

Murphy, Russell D. "Connecticut: Lowell P. Weicker, Jr., A Maverick in the Land of Steady Habits." In Thad Beyle, ed., *Governors and Hard Times*. Washington: Congressional Quarterly Press, 1992.

Purcell, Richard J. *Connecticut in Transition: 1775-1818*. Middletown, CT: Wesleyan University Press, 1963.

Rose, Gary L. *Connecticut Politics at the Crossroads*. Lanham: University Press of America, 1992.

_____. *Connecticut Government at the Millennium*. Fairfield, CT: Sacred Heart University Press, 2001.

_____ed. *Public Policy in Connecticut: Challenges and Perspectives*. Fairfield, CT: Sacred Heart University Press, 2005.

Roth, David M. and Freeman Meyer. *From Revolution to Constitution: Connecticut 1763 to 1818*. Chester, CT: Pequot Press, 1975.

Satter, Robert. *Under the Gold Dome*. New Haven: Connecticut Conference of Municipalities, 2004.

Secretary of State, *Connecticut State Register and Manual*. 2006. www.sots.ct.gov/RegisterManual/regman.ht

Sembor, Edward C. *An Introduction to Connecticut State and Local Government*. Lanham: University Press of America, 2003.

Swanson, Wayne. *Lawmaking in Connecticut: The General Assembly*. New London, CT: Connecticut College, 1978.

Van Dusen, Albert E. *Puritans Against the Wilderness: Connecticut History to 1763*. Chester, CT: Pequot Press, 1975.

Weicker, Lowell P., Jr. *Maverick: A Life in Politics*. Boston: Little Brown, 1995.

White John Kenneth. *The Fractured Electorate: Political Parties and Social Change in Southern New England*. Hanover, NH: University Press of New England, 1983.

Index